The Praxis of English Languag

CRITICAL NEW LITERACIES: THE PRAXIS OF ENGLISH LANGUAGE TEACHING AND LEARNING (PELT)

Volume 1

Series Editors:

Marcelle Cacciattolo, *Victoria University, Australia*
Tarquam McKenna, *Victoria University, Australia*
Shirley Steinberg, *University of Calgary, Canada*
Mark Vicars, *Victoria University, Australia*

As a praxis-based sequence these texts are specifically designed by the team of international scholars to engage in local in-country language pedagogy research. This exciting and innovative series will bring a dynamic contribution to the development of critical new literacies. With a focus on literacy teaching, research methods and critical pedagogy, the founding principle of the series is to investigate the practice of new literacies in English language learning and teaching, as negotiated with relevance to the localized educational context. It is being and working alongside people in the world that is at the core of the PELT viewpoint. The Praxis of English Language Teaching and Learning series will focus on inter-culturality and interdisciplinary qualitative inquiry and the dissemination of "non-colonised" research.

The Praxis of English Language Teaching and Learning (PELT)

Beyond the Binaries: Researching Critically in EFL Classrooms

Edited by

Mark Vicars
Victoria University, Australia

Shirley Steinberg
University of Calgary, Canada

Tarquam McKenna
Victoria University, Australia

and

Marcelle Cacciattolo
Victoria University, Australia

SENSE PUBLISHERS
ROTTERDAM / BOSTON / TAIPEI

A C.I.P. record for this book is available from the Library of Congress.

ISBN 978-94-6300-110-6 (paperback)
ISBN 978-94-6300-111-3 (hardback)
ISBN 978-94-6300-112-0 (e-book)

Published by: Sense Publishers,
P.O. Box 21858,
3001 AW Rotterdam,
The Netherlands
https://www.sensepublishers.com/

Printed on acid-free paper

Contents

Chapter One

Employing the Bricolage as Critical Research in Teaching English as a Foreign Language

SHIRLEY R. STEINBERG

In this chapter, I discuss critical theory and critical social theory in terms of their implications for research and teaching in Teaching English as a Foreign Language (TEFL). I attempt to focus on practical implications of the critical conversation for those interested in critical pedagogy, research, and good teaching in TEFL. The research bricolage is presented in light of viewing ways in which different epistemological research "methodologies" can be employed when doing TEFL research.

The chapter is structured into two sections that focus on (1) a clarification of the nature of critical research and (2) methodologies of critical research, using the bricolage and the implications for TEFL researchers.

Criticalized Research

Critical research makes the assumption that the inequalities of today's society need to be addressed and that the world would be a better place if these unjust realities could be changed. Consequently, we explore the world, TEFL included, for the purpose of exposing this injustice, developing prac-

This chapter was revised from: Steinberg, S.R. & Kincheloe, J. L. (2011). "Employing the bricolage as critical research in science education. In Fraser, B., Tobin, K, & McRobbie, C. (Eds). (2011). *Second International handbook of science education:* Dordrecht: Springer publishers.

M. Vicars et al. (eds.), *The Praxis of English Language Teaching and Learning (PELT)*, 1–19.

tical ways to change it, and identifying sites and strategies by which transformation can be accomplished. Although the notion is simple, the process of accomplishing it is disconcertingly complex. Critical research needs embrace these five notions:

1. It is not rooted in positivism, or notions of rationality, objectivity and truth. Positivist rationality involves the assumption that human beings control their destinies through the application of social techniques derived from empirical science. Through scientific reason, educators, social workers, psychologists and other cultural workers can make use of sciences of control to produce obedient citizens.

2. Critical research attains an awareness of its own value commitments and those of others, as well as the values promoted by dominant culture. One of the main concerns of critical research involves the exposure of the relationship between personal values and practice. Critical research makes its value assumptions known to its consumers (e.g., that English language speaking should be employed for peaceful, socially just and democratic purposes).

3. It cultivates an awareness of the social and political construction of professional consciousness. Critical research understands that academic researchers are socialized into professional cultures with certain mores and expectations. It insists on making public these hidden customs.

4. Critical Research uncovers aspects of the dominant social order that undermine the pursuit of critical egalitarian and democratic goals. It attempts to expose the specific methods upon which power deploys to crush critical objectives in the larger effort to protect its own privileges (e.g., the ways in which corporate and governmental financial support of research often shape the questions which researchers ask and the answers they provide).

5. It is always conceived in relation to practice. Critical research is never disinterested and it exists to improve practice (see Kincheloe and Berry 2004). The employment of a bricolage allows a socially just and polysemic approach in creating thicker textual readings of research.

Critical Traditions

Critical research draws upon emergent schools of social theory. First, Frankfurt School critical theory (a discourse of social transformation) is associated with the work of Max Horkheimer, Theodor Adorno and Herbert Marcuse (many others are part of the Frankfurt School). Second, Michel Foucault's genealogy (the reconstitution of ostensibly mundane historical memories that are dangerous to the dominant way of understanding the world) attempts to understand social practices even when the researcher has been shaped by the social practices). Third, the practice of poststructuralist deconstruction (a method of reading, an interpretive strategy, and a philosophical position that views the world as full of texts to be decoded and explored for unintended meanings) is associated with Jacques Derrida. Fourth, the critical currents (ways of understanding the world that challenge the certainty of modernist science with its linear, cause-effect forms of logic and rationality) associated with critical cultural studies and critical pedagogy.

Using these critical theories in combination with the pragmatic tradition out of which John Dewey's progressive education developed, an oppositional research impulse can emerge. Dewey wrote in the early 20th century about a form of research that consciously challenged the technicist desire for certainty. A notion of critical TEFL research is nurtured by Dewey's notion, as it undercuts mainstream educational comfort with taken-for-granted sociocultural and educational patterns. In a dominant culture that has not always valued self-reflection on the part of its teacher professionals, critical research becomes a de facto oppositional activity as it pushes professionals in a variety of fields to reconsider their assumptions (Greene 1988). Kincheloe and Berry (2004) argue that critical forms of inquiry do not claim truth in a way that is unaware of the metaphors that guide their meaning. Indeed, such critical research forms do not conceive knowledge as simply something to be discovered. Information produced by critical inquiry, a self-conscious social text is produced by a plethora of mutually-informing contexts. This concern for context becomes a defining feature of critical research, as practitioners focus their effort on conceiving new ways of contextualizing scientific knowledge, teaching and students. The critical theory of TEFL research and teaching is often influenced by a governing body intent on the neo-liberal imposition of English language teaching, and most often ignores any social text whatsoever. In the case of Asian TEFL education, I have found that socio-cultural education, criticality, deconstruction, or social consciousness is non-existent. Indeed, the only goal is to sell English materials from the UK, Australia or New Zealand, most of which include cultural information directly from the authoring country, and not the country engaged in the teaching. Students are taught in rudimentary, rationalistic, positivistic and anti-social manners to regurgitate classes into empirical exams.

Empowerment Through Acknowledgment of Power and Oppression

As critical theory is grounded on the recognition of the ways in which power oppresses, the forces of oppression have to be identified (Kincheloe and Steinberg 2008). In the context of critical research in TEFL, one of the first places where critical inquirers might look for oppression is positivist English language teaching itself. Critical observers have maintained that prediction and control of external phenomena are presupposed in the language of foreign language teaching, science, mathematics, and statistics. The external phenomena in question involve the control of nature to serve human ends (Aronowitz 1988). *Modernist TEFL is committed to expansionism or growth, which are terms that frequently are confused with progress.* In the case of most English language teaching, the goals are *to become global,* and *to speak English in order to be competitive in international markets.* Expansionism of this type demands that individuals be programmed for the progress-oriented agenda even when it conflicts with their best interests or the best interests of the community. *Modernist TEFL is committed to the production of profit and measurement.* Too often, ideas, commodities and people themselves are evaluated in light of their relation to profits. The obsession with instrumental rationality and measurement defines the goals and outcomes of traditional TEFL education. When individuals engage in actions that are contrary to the interests of profit making, empiricism tends to reshape their behavior by labeling it as "soft" research. Finally, most TEFL study is committed to the preservation of bureaucratic structures, which are maintained by "scientifically proven" measurements. Empirical research serves as the force that processes people in relation to the smooth functioning needs of bureaucracies. It is the bureaucratic need, not the human need, which takes precedence when a conflict arises. In a democratic context, critical teacher researchers decide what needs to be learned and discovered in their classes, how such experiences might contribute to sophisticated thinking necessary to democratic citizenship, how to help children learn it, how English can fit *into and* with a native tongue and culture, and how such learning might then be assessed. In a positivistic system we know that the quality of our teaching, our research, and student learning will be tested and measured even if it is never clearly specified what exactly constitutes the purpose of testing. Even if the tests serve to fragment, narrow, deflect, and trivialize the curriculum, we still must use them because accurate scientific measurement takes precedence over such curricular considerations. This positivistic obsession with measurement, exemplified by the high-stakes testing, and the discourse of top-down standards, forces us to assume for the sake of testing efficiency that there is a specific body of knowledge to be learned, and there are correct methods for teaching and learning it.

Positivist TESL instruction/research forces us to unquestioningly accept the validity of the specific body of knowledge to be learned and that such truth belongs in our classrooms. Teachers and educational researchers need not trouble themselves with inquiry about the constituent interests of this knowledge. Educational researchers need only concern themselves with empirical investigations of how best to teach this information. If we manipulate this variable in this specific way, do students acquire more or less of the knowledge? Thus, many would argue, educational issues in this positivistic framework are reduced to technical issues. Questions of ends or purposes are subservient to questions of means or techniques. Critical theorists have labeled this tendency "instrumental rationality." Advocates of critical qualitative approaches to educational research argue that the purpose of educational activity must always be an integral aspect of the research process (Kincheloe and Berry 2004).

Much of TEFL research and teaching searches for results driven by the desire to make large profits through courses, claiming to the students that they will learn English and make large profits through global interaction. This becomes a force of domination not because of its intrinsic truthfulness, but because of the social authority (power) that it brings with it. Expressions such as "researchers contend," "research has proven" and "the test results tell us" signify a power difficult to counter. Critical observers are quick to warn their audiences not to perceive this concept too simplistically. The way in which positivist TEFL research exerts its power is often subtle and rarely takes place without eliciting resistance. Many of the instructors do not have graduate work in the TEFL field, often teaching with a quickly acquired certificate, or assigned courses at the last minute. The field itself, suffers from low esteem, as it is not considered scholarly, nor even pedagogical in nature. The shape and nature of TEFL administration and course design should be analyzed by informed researchers who refuse to allow grand ideological pronouncements to substitute for specific inquiry.

An example is the way in which an unexamined scientism subverts our attempts at democracy. With the increase of environmental hazards resulting from scientific "progress," citizens sometimes seek to legitimate a "totalitarianism of hazard prevention" (Beck 1992, p. 80). In the attempt to prevent something bad (environmental side effects), something worse (suspension of democratic principles) is produced. In this context, the population is divided along a new set of axes—expert versus non-expert, or those who possess the language and methodology of modernist scientific research versus those who don't. The mass of non-experts, the experts maintain, must be provided with technical details that will condition them to respect the magic of the scientific elite. The cultivation of such respect is tantamount to a pacification program designed to quell public protest, criticism or resistance (i.e., to disempower and depoliticise). Use of media has been employed to create populist narratives geared to "simplifying" this scientific research. We saw the global warming debate reduced to Al Gore's sophisticated PowerPoint documentary, and naturally, a backlash politically funded and fought on partisan grounds, which continues years later.

Such an example of anti-democratic scientism highlights the empowerment impulse in critical research. Inquiry that aspires to critical status is connected to the larger effort to confront various kinds of anti-democratic impulses, especially those embedded in the discourse of science. Such research thus becomes a transformative effort unembarrassed by the label "political" and unafraid to consummate a relationship with an emancipatory consciousness. Emancipatory consciousness involves the attempt to free oneself from the tacit controls of racial, class-based and gendered discourses and lived practices. Horkheimer (1972) succinctly argued that critical research has never been satisfied with merely increasing the knowledge base. Therefore, a critical rendition of TEFL research attempts not simply to understand the dynamics of English language teaching and pedagogy, but the interesting ways in which they intersect. Also, TEFL education research attempts to change English language teaching and pedagogy by moving them into the emancipatory domain. Critical TEFL researchers use their work to empower English language educators to construct their practice along well-analyzed moral, ethical and political principles.

English language teachers who enter schools with such understandings and research abilities are prepared to make a cognitive leap. Indeed, the stage has been set to move to postformal thinking (Kincheloe 1995). As critical researchers with a vision of "what could be" and a mechanism for uncovering "what is," these teachers see the sociopolitical contradictions of both language teaching and schools in a concrete manner. Such recognitions encourage reflection as they induce teachers to understand how these sociopolitical distortions tacitly have worked to shape their worldviews and self-perceptions. With a deeper understanding of such processes, practitioners recognize the ways in which power operates to create oppressive conditions for some groups and privilege for others. Thus, critical research opens new ways of knowing that transcend formal analysis (Steinberg 2006; Kincheloe and Berry 2004; Horn 2000).

Critical Pedagogical Research in TEFL

Critical social research (in the critical pedagogical/theoretical sense) can be labeled as "hyperreal"—this implies researching an information society which is socially saturated with ever-increasing forms of representation (e.g., filmic, photographic and electronic) all of which have had a profound effect on constructing the cultural narratives that shape our identities. The drama of living has been portrayed so often on television that individuals are increasingly able to predict the outcomes to be the "natural" and "normal" course of social life (Gergen 1991). As many critical cultural studies analysts have put it, we become pastiches or imitative conglomerations of one another. Our emotional bonds are diffused as social media assaults us with representations that have shaped our cognitive and affective facilities in ways that still remain insufficiently understood. The need for immediate communication gratification has plunged the linked in, connected, wired masses in such a way that education is usurped by non-theoretical, non-professional commentary, and a viral curriculum becomes the dominant discourse (Steinberg 2009). An example of a postmodern media event was clear in the 2014 Ebola culture of fear created by tweets, Facebook and mainstream news stations creating feeds based on those viral announcements of the spread of epidemic. News became saturated with news about news, news from social network sites, and as afterthoughts, doctors and researchers were brought in to discuss the possible epidemic. And, back to production of capital and profit, the "experts" employed also presented agenda-ridden commentaries, depending on their political, ideological stances, or on which pharmaceutical company's press releases and research were being used.

It is misleading merely to identify postmodernism (the philosophical critique) and critical research bricolage with poststructuralism. Poststructuralism has attacked the premises and assumptions of structuralism and its attempt to create a scientific basis for the study of culture. Grounded on a firm belief in certainty and objectivity, structuralists posited that an unchanging and fixed human nature existed and could be described accurately by scientific methods. For example, intelligence was fixed and could be precisely measured by IQ tests. Poststructuralists have denied the existence of scientific certainty, arguing that human identity and consciousness are historically produced. Therefore, identity and consciousness take on different forms in different eras (Best and Kellner 1991). In this context, there are many similarities between postmodernism, postructuralism, and critical bricolage but they differ as to their referents. Postmodernism (the critique) is an umbrella category pertaining to a range of philosophical positions that critique the modernist thought produced in Western societies during and after the Enlightenment. Poststructuralism is an academic discourse that subverts particular scientific practices that assumed an unproblematic representation of the nature of reality. Poststructuralism is a critical postmodernist discourse, but not all critical or postmodern expressions are postructuralist. Critical bricolage can simplistically appear as a mixed-research methodology. While, indeed, different "methodologies" are employed, bricolage cloaks itself within a critical theoretical commitment to social justice and a critical pedagogical underpinning combining theory, discourse, identity, and the political.

The critical research bricolage I am proposing is not only based on critique. The synergism of the conversation between the research bricolage and critical theory involves an interplay between the praxis of the critical and the radical uncertainty of what is often referred to as the postmodern. As it invokes its emancipatory strategies for the emancipation of meaning, critical theoretical bricolage provides the postmodern critique with a normative foundation (i.e., a basis for distinguishing between oppressive and liberatory social relations). Without such a foundation, the postmodern critique is vulnerable to nihilism and inaction. Indeed, normatively ungrounded postmodern critique is incapable of providing an ethically challenging and politically transformative program of action. I argue that, if the critical pedagogical (postmodern) critique is to make a valuable contribution to the notion of schooling as an emancipatory form of cultural politics, it must make connections to those egalitarian impulses of modernism that contribute to an emancipatory democracy. In doing this, the project of an emancipatory democracy and the schooling that supports it can be extended by new understandings of how power operates and by incorporating groups who had been excluded by their race, gender, sexuality, abledness, religion, or class (Kincheloe and Steinberg 2008).

Critical research has never been reluctant to point out the limitations of empirical research, calling attention to the inability of traditional models of inquiry to escape the boundaries of a narrative realism. However, the research bricolage *does not* exclude empirical work, indeed, certain data can only serve to further the thickening of the tentative interpretation by the researcher. Certainly, in TEFL research and teaching, there is a place for quantitative data. The rigorous methodological approaches of empirical inquiry often preclude larger interpretations of the forces that shape both the researcher and the researched. Empirical observation cannot supplant theoretical analysis and critical reflection. The project of critical research is not simply the empirical representation of the world but the transgressive task of posing research itself as a set of ideological practices. Empirical analysis

needs to be interrogated in order to uncover the contradictions and nega-
tions embodied in any objective description. Critical researchers maintain
that the meaning of an experience or an observation is not self-evident. The
meaning of any experience depends on the struggle over the interpretation
and definition of that experience (Weiler 1988).

The ways in which we analyze and interpret empirical data are conditioned by the theoretically frames used and dependent on the researcher's
own ideological assumptions. The empirical data derived from any study
cannot be treated as simple irrefutable facts. The employment of instrumen-
tally rational positivist readings of data does not serve to present any type
of truth except the "truth" which is predetermined by the researcher (due to
the choice of methodology and positivist reading). They represent hidden
assumptions, which the critical researcher must dig out and expose. As Einstein and Heisenberg pointed out long ago, what we see is not what we see
but what we perceive (Kincheloe, Steinberg and Tippins 1999). The knowledge that the world yields has to be interpreted by men and women who
are a part of that world. What we call information always involves an act of
human judgment. From a critical perspective, this act of judgment or interpretation is a theoretical act (Kincheloe 1991). Critical analysts contend that
theory involves understanding the relationship between the particular and
the whole and between the subject and the object of analysis. Such a position contradicts the traditional empiricist contention that theory is basically
a matter of classifying objective data.

Cultural Studies in Critical TEFL Teaching and Research

Over the last three decades, cultural studies' popularity has increased in uni-
versities throughout the world. As an interdisciplinary, transdisciplinary and
sometimes counter-disciplinary field, cultural studies functions within the
dynamics of competing definitions of culture. Rather than equating culture
with high culture, cultural studies asserts that myriad expressions of cultural
production should be analyzed in relation to other cultural dynamics and
social and historical structures. Attempting to connect critical theory with
the particularity of everyday experience, students of cultural studies argue
that all experience is vulnerable to ideological inscription. At the same time,

researchers maintained that theorizing outside of everyday experience results in formal and deterministic theory.

While cultural studies are associated with the study of popular culture, it is not primarily *about* popular culture. Cultural studies is broader and involves the production and nature of the rules of inclusivity and exclusivity that guide academic evaluation, particularly the way in which these rules shape and are shaped by relations of power. Such insights are especially important for research in science education, as they allow insights into scientific assumptions typically outside the purview of the field (Steinberg 2006).

Like any critical field of research, cultural studies is concerned with its application to the world outside the academy. Proponents maintain that cultural studies should address the most urgent social questions of the day in the most rigorous intellectual manner available. Thus, the everyday concerns of cultural studies are contextually bound. So important is this notion of context that some scholars label the work of cultural studies as "radical contextualism." As Emdin (2009) noted, researchers should also understand that the popular and the contextual often leads to better research and certainly better pedagogy.

In my own work as a professor in EFL, it was essential for me to begin my classes with auto-ethnographical writings done by my students. After we inquired into self, we began to draw connections with personal and public culture within the students' own environments. The study of Vietnamese or Thai popular culture followed, along with the political and critical theoretical study of the colonial influences of English within the Asian cultures. As my students began to understand the *reasons* they *had* to learn English, they also understood the oppressive nature of the way in which traditional English language had been taught. This understanding brought about an empowerment as to the nature and place of the English language, along with high quality, rich texted, bricolaged research and writing.

Engaging the Bricolage

This section starts by discussing the need for the critical researcher to be comfortable in choosing from a wide range of critical postmodern research methods. Then, detailed consideration is given to two critical scientific methods: semiotics and critical ethnography.

Critical research in TEFL education can make no guarantee about what particular questions will be important in varying contexts, one methodology cannot be privileged over others; at the same time, none can be eliminated without due examination. Ethnography, textual analysis, semiotics, deconstruction, critical hermeneutics, interviews, phonemic analysis, psychoanalysis, rhizomatics, content analysis, survey research and phenomenology only begin a list of methods which a critical researcher might bring to the table (Steinberg 2006; Kincheloe and Berry 2004). Such an eclectic view of research has been labeled *bricolage* (Denzin and Lincoln 1994), which involves taking research strategies from a variety of disciplines and traditions as they are needed in the unfolding context of the research situation. Such a position is pragmatic and strategic and demands self-consciousness and an awareness of context from the researcher. Borrowing from the term coined by Claude Levi-Strauss, Denzin and Lincoln allude to the possibilities engaged by creating a multi-layered complex research methodology.

The critical researcher is able to negotiate a panoply of data gathering techniques and a plethora of interpretive theoretical constructs (e.g., feminism, Marxism, cultural studies, critical constructivism, critical theory, critical/resistance postmodernism). Most critical methods can be deployed at some point in one context or another to achieve critical postmodern goals. Such efforts hinge on the researchers' theoretical understanding of the critical tradition and their ability to apply this understanding to the social and interpersonal aspects of her life (e.g., understanding the relationship between one's "way of seeing" and the race, class and gender location of personal history). In appreciating research as a political act, the critical bricoleur abandons the quest for objectivity and instead focuses on the clarification of the values that he or she brings to the inquiry (Denzin and Lincoln 1994). Following are two examples of qualitative "methodology" which can be combined within a bricolaged approach.

Semiotics

A couple of examples of critical methods in education are in order. Semiotics is the study of codes and signs that help humans derive meaning from their surroundings. TEFL researchers can use semiotic methods to gain insights into deep structures moving classroom events. Indeed, classrooms are gold mines for semiotic study for they abound in codes, signs and conventions that call for unique insight. My English language students (who were, themselves teachers of English) would spend a full day walking through the downtown marketplace of their own city. They were asked to look for English words and phrases. When I assigned the exercise the first time, they laughed and insisted there was no English in Hanoi or Ho Chi Minh City. After hours of walking and talking, recording, and taking photos, they met to discuss their findings. The discussion itself, became semiotic. Within minutes of describing and categorizing what they saw (the signs), with lightening speed, they began to make phenomenological and hermeneutic observations:

Why was there so much English found?

Who was being represented in advertisements?

Why were Western, White models used in so store windows in a city which has few visitors and even less European residents?

How was English used to mock, imitate, or reduce Vietnamese context?

What was being colonized in these advertisements?

Why would stores use English when none of the workers knew one word of English?

What is read between the lines in the promotion of goods in English?

What does it mean to find English in a Vietnamese context?

How has English colonialism replaced the French context in Vietnam?

In a Communist country, how has capitalism become a dominant signifier through the English language?

Critical researchers of the profound in the mundane begin to move beyond traditional questions of teaching to inquiries about who are we becoming as a result of this education experience (Britzman 1991).

Semiotics makes the given an object of thought and critical focus. Semiotics refuses the shallowness of lived experience, as it searches for ways of seeing that describe the invisible. Viewed from this perspective of the critical, an emancipatory EFL class involves far more than a set of enrichment activities for the smarter children. Levels of obscured assumptions begin to jump out of such programs when the light of grounded critique is shone upon them. Thus, research moves from the glorification of the novel to the analysis of the assumed. In this context, language transcends its role as conduit for information. Semiotic analysts view the relationship between speaker and listener or writer and reader to be based on constant interpretation in the context of the semiotic matrices brought to the act of communication by all participants. Thus, communication becomes not a matter of extracting meaning from communiqués, but of constituting meaning based on the cultural context, values and social identities of those involved (Manning and Cullum-Swan 1994).

When researchers turn such interpretive strategies upon their own practice, they engage in semiotics of introspection. As researchers analyze their actions with attention to ritual, metaphor and questioning strategies, they uncover hidden dimensions of their belief structures, their familiar cognitive strategies, their assumptions about students, and their attitudes towards the "proper" deportment of a teacher (Courteney 1988). No longer can knowledge producers hide in the shelter of the Cartesian-Newtonian objectivism, which shields them from the personal issues associated with all educational acts. Semiotic researchers cannot view themselves as transhistorical beings— they need to understand their place in the web from which they see reality. Contextualized in this way, the schemata, the values and the belief structures that defy recognition as they fade in the familiarity of our consciousness are highlighted as the ink of semiotics dyes them. Historical contextualization of self in this situation utilizes the insight of difference, as we finally begin to see ourselves when we are placed against a social backdrop of values and ways of perceiving that are unfamiliar (Kellner 1991).

Critical Ethnography

Critical ethnography is another example of a critical research methodology that can be adapted to the bricolage. Ethnography (the study of events as they evolve in their natural setting) often is described as the most basic form of social research. While ethnographers disagree over the relative importance of each purpose, ethnography attempts to gain knowledge about a particular culture, to identify patterns of social interaction, and to develop holistic in-

terpretations of societies and social institutions. Thus, ethnography in education attempts to understand the nature of schools and other educational
agencies in these ways, and seeks to appreciate the social processes, which
move educational events. Ethnography attempts to make explicit the assumptions, which one takes for granted as a culture member. The culture
could be as broad as Japanese culture or as narrow as a humble child from a
fishing village. The critical ethnographer seeks to describe the concrete experiences of everyday language teaching/speaking or educational life and the
social patterns, which construct it. One of the most basic tools of the critical
researcher is derived from the ethnographic tradition (Clough 1992).

Critical forms of ethnography have focused on the discontinuities, contradictions, and inconsistencies of cultural expression and human action. As
opposed to modernist forms of ethnography, postmodern methods refuse
the attempt to reconcile the differences once and for all. The postmodern
critique of classical ethnography highlights the tendency of the tradition to
privilege a dominant narrative and a unitary, privileged vantage point. In the
effort to conflate knower and known, the postmodern ethnographer pro-
poses a dialogue between the researcher and the researched that attempts to
smash traditional hierarchical relations between them (Atkinson and Hammersley 1994). In the process, the modernist notion of ethnography as an
instrument of enlightenment and civilization of the "native" *objects* of study
dies an overdue death. Critical ethnographies are texts to be argued over
whose meanings are never "natural" but are constructed by circumstance.
Such characteristics obviously are colored by postmodern ethnography's ren-
dezvous with contemporary literacy criticism and its Derridian influences
(Aronowitz 1993).

Bricoleurs

By using the examples of semiotics and ethnography as two research concepts
that can be employed with a bricolaged methodology, I introduce the notion
of rigor through the blending various qualitative methods to create a deep
reading and interpretation of research. The bricolage is a critical approach,
which understands that the frontiers of knowledge work best in the liminal
zones where disciplines collide. Thus, in the deep interdisciplinarity of the

bricolage researchers learn to engage in a form of boundary work. Such scholarly labor involves establishing diverse networks and conferences where synergistic interactions can take place as proponents of different methodologies, students of divergent subject matters, and individuals confronted with different problems interact. In this context, scholars learn across these domains and educate intermediaries who can build bridges between various territories. As disciplinary intermediaries operating as bricoleurs facilitate this boundary work, they create conceptual and electronic links that help researchers in different domains interact. If the cutting edge of research lives at the intersection of disciplinary borders, then developing the bricolage is a key strategy in the development of rigorous and innovative research. The facilitation and cultivation of boundary work is a central element of this process.

There is nothing simple about conducting research at the interdisciplinary frontier in English language teaching. Many scholars report that the effort to develop expertise in different disciplines and research methodologies demands more than a casual acquaintance with the literature of a domain. In this context there is a need for personal interaction between representatives from diverse disciplinary domains and scholarly projects to facilitate these encounters. Many researchers find it extremely difficult to make sense of "outside" fields and the more disciplines a researcher scans the harder the process becomes. If the scholar does not have access to historical dimensions of the field, the contexts that envelope the research methods used and the knowledge produced in the area, or contemporary currents involving debates and controversies in the discipline, the boundary work of the bricolage becomes exceedingly frustrating and futile. Proponents of the bricolage must help develop specific strategies for facilitating this complicated form of scholarly labor.

In this context we come to understand that a key aspect of "doing bricolage" involves the development of conceptual tools for boundary work. Such tools might include the promotion and cultivation of detailed reviews of research in a particular domain written with the needs of bricoleurs in mind. Researchers from a variety of disciplinary domains should develop information for bricolage projects. Hypertextual projects that provide conceptual matrices for bringing together diverse literatures, examples of data produced by different research methods, connective insights, and bibliographic compilations can be undertaken by bricoleurs with the help of information professionals. Such projects would integrate a variety of conceptual understandings including the previously mentioned historical, contextual, and contemporary currents of disciplines (Freidman 1998).

Doug Kellner (1991) is helpful in this context with his argument that multiperspectival approaches to research may not be very helpful unless the object of inquiry and the various methods used to study it are situated historically. In this way the forces operating to socially construct all elements of the research process are understood, an appreciation that leads to a grasp of new relationships and connections. Such an appreciation opens new interpretive windows that lead to more rigorous modes of analysis and interpretation. This historicization of the research and the researched is an intrinsic aspect of the bricolage and the education of the bricoleur. Since learning to become a bricoleur is a lifelong process, what I am discussing here relates to the lifelong curriculum for preparing bricoleurs.

Also necessary to this boundary work and the education of the bricoleur are social-theoretical and hermeneutical understandings. Social theory alerts bricoleurs to the implicit assumptions within particular approaches to research and the ways they shape their findings. With grounding in social theory bricoleurs can make more informed decisions about the nature of the knowledge produced in the field and how researchers discern the worth of the knowledge they themselves produce. With the benefit of hermeneutics, bricoleurs are empowered to synthesize data collected via multiple methods. In the hermeneutic process this ability to synthesize diverse information moves the bricoleur to a more sophisticated level of meaning making (Foster 1997). Life on the disciplinary boundaries is never easy, but the rewards to be derived from the hard work demanded are profound.

Teaching/Researching English for Foreign Learners

Critical research bricolage, and the educational forms emerging from it assume that TEFL educators must understand the conditions and effects of knowledge production, while engaging in knowledge production themselves. In the present regime, this strikes us as a difficult or insurmountable task. Given my experiences with TEFL educators and foreign English language students and the brilliance, which they bring to their tasks, I believe that such understandings are possible. As knowledge producers, English language educators can weave understandings of knowledge validation, student experience and the notion of consciousness construction with the latest research in, say, quantum physics or molecular biology. Students can be introduced to the ethnographic, semiotic, phenomenological, critical hermeneutical, deconstructive and psychoanalytical dimensions of the bricolage in the process of coming to understand the social, political and epistemological forces that shape language learning, education and their lives in general. In this context, English educators gain the ability to step back from the world and look at it anew. In seeing from a perspective different from the one to which they have been conditioned, TEFL educators uncover new vantage points to observe the constructing forces (Adler 1991). As they produce knowledge, they remake their professional lives and they rename their worlds.

Dr. Shirley R. Steinberg
Werklund School of Education
University of Calgary

References

Adler, S. (1991). Forming a critical pedagogy in the social studies methods class: The use of imaginative literature. In B. Tabuchnick & K. Zeichner (eds.), *Issues and practices in inquiry-oriented teacher education* (pp. 77-90). New York: Falmer Press.

Aronowitz, S. (1988). *Science as power: Discourse and ideology in modern society.* Minneapolis, MN: University of Minnesota Press.

Aronowitz, S. (1993). *Roll over Beethoven: The return of cultural strife.* Hanover, NH: Wesleyan University Press.

Atkinson, P., & Hammersley, M. (1994). Ethnography and participant observation. In N. Denzin & Y. Lincoln (eds.), *Handbook of qualitative research* (pp. 248-261). Thousand Oakes, CA: Sage.

Beck, U. (1992). *Risk society: Towards a new modernity* (translated by M. Ritter). London: Sage.

Best, S., & Kellner, D. (1991). *Postmodern theory: Critical interrogations.* New York: Guilford Press.

Bohm, D., & Peat, F. (1987). *Science, order, and creativity.* New York: Bantam Books.

Britzman, D. (1991). *Practice makes practice: A critical study of learning to teach.* Albany, NY: State University of New York Press.

Clough, P. (1992). *The end(s) of ethnography: From realism to social criticism.* Newbury Park, CA: Sage.

Courteney, R. (1988). *No one way of being: A study of the practical knowledge of elementary arts teachers.* Toronto, Canada: MGS Publications.

Denzin, N., & Lincoln, Y. (1994). Introduction: Entering the field of qualitative research. In N. Denzin & Y. Lincoln (eds.), *Handbook of qualitative research* (pp. 1-17). Thousand Oakes, CA: Sage.

Emdin, C. (2009). Reality pedagogy: Hip Hop culture and the Urban classroom. In W.M. Roth (ed.). *Science education from people for people: Taking a stand(point).* New York: Routledge.

Gergen, K. (1991). *The saturated self: Dilemmas of identity in contemporary life.* New York: Basic Books.

Greene, M. (1988). *The dialectic of freedom.* New York: Teachers College Press.

Horn, R. (2000). *Teacher talk: A post-formal inquiry into educational change.* New York: Peter Lang Publishing.

Horkheimer, M. (1972). *Critical theory.* New York: Seabury.

Kellner, D. (1991). Reading images critically: Toward a postmodern pedagogy. In H. Giroux (ed.), *Postmodernism, feminism, and cultural politics: Redrawing educational boundaries* (pp. 60-82). Albany, NY: State University of New York Press.

Kincheloe, J. (1991). *Teachers as researchers: Qualitative paths to empowerment.* New York: Falmer.

Kincheloe, J. (1995). *Toil and trouble: Good work, smart workers, and the integration of academic and vocational education.* New York: Peter Lang.

Kincheloe, J., & Berry, K. (2004). *Rigour and complexity in educational research: Conceptualizing the bricolage.* London: Open University Press.

Kincheloe, J., & Steinberg, S. (2008). Indigenous Knowledges in Education: Complexities, Dangers, and Profound Benefits. In Handbook of Critical Indigenous Methodologies, N. Denzin, Y. Lincoln, & L. Smith (eds.), Thousand Oaks, CA: Sage Publishing.

Kincheloe, J., Steinberg, S., & Tippins, D. (1999). *The stigma of genius: Einstein, consciousness, and education.* New York: Peter Lang Publishing.

Leshan, L., & Margenau, H. (1982). *Einstein's space and Van Gogh's sky: Physical reality and beyond.* New York: Macmillan.

Mahoney, M., & Lyddon, W. (1988). Recent developments in cognitive approaches to counseling and psychotherapy, *The Counseling Psychologist* 16, 190-234.

Manning, P., & Cullum-Swan, B. (1994). Narrative, content, and semiotic analysis. In N. Denzin & Y. Lincoln (eds.), *Handbook of qualitative research* (pp. 463-477). Thousand Oaks, CA: Sage.

Steinberg, S. (2006). Critical Cultural Studies Research: Bricolage in Action. In K. Tobin & J. L. Kincheloe (eds.), *Doing Educational Research.* Rotterdam: Sense Publishers.

Weiler, K. (1988). *Women teaching for change.* South Hadley, MA: Bergin and Garvey.

West, C. (1991). *The ethical dimensions of Marxist thought.* New York: Monthly Review Press.

Chapter Two

Encounter and Dialogue in EFL Classrooms

Interculturalism in Praxis

DOMENICA MAVIGLIA

In 1964, McLuhan predicted a series of phenomena linked to the advent of the so-called 'global village', such as 'globalization', 'new economy' and 'information technology revolutions'. Today, these phenomena are still causing a strong physical, intellectual, and cultural nomadism that involves unprecedented moments of confrontation between individuals on an ethnic, linguistic, and cultural level. This process has led to the creation of current multi-ethnic and multi-cultural societies. Besides, it has prompted an existential ambiguity due to the simultaneous desire of staying where someone feels a real sense of belonging and, at the same time, the need of 'going away'. In this chapter, this nomadism is explored in the context of EFL classrooms and in relation to the contemporary challenge of bringing together individual peculiarities with universal features, combining local and global aspects. The pedagogical task resulting from this process requires to avoid an oppressive standardization, a phenomenon that denies the possibility of being 'different' or thinking 'in another way'; and at the same time it requires to keep the rightful protection of individual peculiarities away from

M. Vicars et al. (eds.), *The Praxis of English Language Teaching and Learning (PELT)*, 21–37.

the traps of localism or the glorification of one's roots, attitudes that can lead to harmful kinds of 'identity obsession', main cause of violent divisions, clashes, and discriminations (Pinto Minerva 2002).

This chapter aims therefore at highlighting the teleological value of the critical-intercultural education that takes place in EFL classrooms and its role as promoter of a 'humanizing' path that rediscovers, respects, and recognizes the true face of the Other as individual and resource, making it a completely different process compared to all possible forms of hidden cultural neocolonialism.

Interculturalism in EFL Classrooms: The Praxis of Encounter and Dialogue

In today's complex and continuously changing society, the importance of the dialogical-intercultural approach in the field of pedagogy is under careful investigation. The dialogical-intercultural approach highlights the salience of mutual respect and recognition of otherness and eliminates the use of hierarchical categories, in order to promote a pedagogical encounter that creates relationships and synthesis among differences.

Today's globalized world is composed of so many cultures that there is an increasing need to adopt an intercultural approach. The value and functionality of this approach is linked to the fact that it represents a new and disrupting device to understand how teaching and learning in EFL classrooms can create a maieutic-educational space open to engagement, dialogue, and understanding. In other words, a space that boasts the potential of creating a new *modus vivendi* which requires the acquisition of a new mentality that goes beyond the limits of sense of belonging and opens up, instead, to the resources of a space of cultural pluralism.

According to Franco Cambi, the current generation 'must devise a series of strategies to evaluate and review interculturalism in its whole complexity, integrity, and in its articulated and dysmorphic physiognomy' (Cambi 2006, p. 15). Interculturalism is therefore to be considered as a theoretical model and a historical-social objective. It must be tackled as a challenge to mental habits, prejudices, cognitive and axiological criteria. It should help us overcome identities without nullifying them and bring us in a new moral universe built on encounter and dialogue. A universe where the rule is to interact with and develop common spaces that respect difference and its value. It is important to recognize, strengthen, articulate and support this idea of interculturalism (Cambi 2006, p. 7).

As it becomes clearer and clearer that our societies are becoming more and more multicultural, it is more and more urgent for this multiculturalism to turn into an interculturalism characterized by encounter, dialogue, engagement, and understanding in a climate of diversity, but where difference is respected. Clearly, interculturalism is a challenge in itself: it goes against the common mental habits of the average Western and European man, but also against cultures in general, since they normally are defensive and ready to fight against the 'enemy' model. On the one hand, interculturalism requires therefore a new *forma mentis*, which should be pluralistic, dynamic, and open. On the other hand, it requires also a new *ethos*, which should be dialogical and fair.

Therefore, as previously stated, interculturalism requires a 'space of encounter', a complex and dynamic space that should be carefully built and protected, hence pedagogically managed. In this landscape still in the making (*in fieri*), pedagogy represents, both at a community and individual level, the best means to promote a change in mentalities, relationships, roles of the economy or of the states; while at the same time, it declares and supports values, attitudes, and mental habits that should be implemented with time. This kind of pedagogy should aim at guarding against possible drifts or dangerous forms of pessimism, to relaunch instead an axiological, critical, and even utopian idea of pedagogy, which could tackle and unveil the defects and lacks of functional, technical, adaptive, and conformist pedagogy.

As a matter of fact, interculturalism is one of the key pedagogical devices of our age, an era characterized by globalization, pluralism, and difference. This age requires a pedagogy that must be able to take on the challenge represented by the difficult, open, and flexible structures that are still in the making and keep getting renovated in contemporary life. Interculturalism deserves therefore a structural 'place' in the current educational system. It is indeed a challenge rooted in multicultural societies, but it is also a pedagogical exercise that defies the typical mentalities and identities of monocultures by relaunching values like dialogue, peace, and solidarity as basis to build a cognitive and moral education that could provide the sound and useful foundations needed to support the new rules of societal co-existence. 'A global society rocked by deep and shocking injustices; terrible inequalities; asymmetrical lifestyles and rights; a too-much-widespread, sneaky and repetitive barbarity' (Cambi 2006, p. 8). As previously stated, interculturalism is the creation of a new frame of mind, free of all ethnocentric concepts and instead dialogical, open to listening to the other, and ready for the encounter. A new, unstructured frame of mind that sees the mixing of cultures as a resource. Nevertheless, this type of mindset is not easy to create, assimilate, embrace, and use in daily life and social activities. In other words, as Franco Cambi (2006) explains, to activate and trigger this new frame of mind it is necessary, on the one hand, to employ some key concepts of cultural anthropology, like the autonomy of cultures, relativism, pluralism, non-hierarchization; and on the other hand, to employ pedagogy with the aim of bringing to the society and its individuals the principles/values of dialogue, understanding, deconstructionism, and solidarity, which are the engine and result of the 'space of encounter'.

Today, it is therefore necessary to consider the 'space of encounter' as the key factor of the educational and pedagogical effort that interculturalism entails; a theoretical and practical effort to raise awareness, create new models, promote introspection, and create a new way of 'stay in' and 'live' a culture. A training and educational effort that involves individuals, communities, and cultures that 'encounter' and 'live' the complex and dialectic space represented, for example, by EFL classrooms.

All this leads to the conclusion that the 'space of encounter' is a space distinctly pedagogic, built through educational practices and fully expressed in the theory of education. Therefore, this space resembles an endless building site, always in the making. 'It is a space that must be protected and built, devised and wanted; built, devised and wanted as a space inhabited by individuals that can be educated right there, find there their places, change, develop a *habitus* and an identity; and at the same time the space must assign them a place, identity, and meaning. A space that is simultaneously educational and pedagogical, where an intercultural practice is implemented and there is a theory of interculturalism, and where these elements interact with each other to influence the individuals, cultures, institutions, and social groups, changing their identity processes and their sense of belonging' (Cambi 2006, p. 27).

The intercultural interpretation given to the dialogical approach of the education effort described above might represent a true breakaway from the past and it might turn the risky and troubling multiethnic and multicultural co-existence into a growth and enrichment opportunity. In the current era characterized by a crisis of values and a widespread sense of disorientation, it is crucial to point out the topicality and urgency of a thorough pedagogic reflection and recognize the value of critical-intercultural education. This acquires even a bigger importance in the practice of education in every situation, for example in the context of FFL classrooms.

In this situation of historic renewal and fight between different cultural models that originate forms of racism, ethnic closure and fundamentalism; the Western world must recognize its duty, necessity, and main objective: recalibrate itself to get away from centuries of domination, colonialism, and self-celebration, while moving instead towards pluralism and diversity, assigning a crucial and decisive role to education. The educational effort must be widespread and capillary to make it possible to design and build new values, new mindsets, new social co-existence models, the development of individuals, and the collaboration among people and cultures.

In this brand-new framework that only recently has started to be implemented, only education can lead to the creation of a globalization process that can build the 'common foundations' of that future world where we are already living, as individual and groups. Nevertheless, this will be possible only if we consider education as an educational effort carried out among individuals and communities to raise their awareness and help them shouldering their responsibilities in a culture of dialogue and recognition, as part of a real empowering process. Only education 'can save us', because its processes are the only ones that can foster a change *in interiore homine*. Because only education has the possibility to work on that thin and complex line that transforms values, models, and mindsets; devising and implementing 'anthropologic changes'.

Pedagogy must therefore take on the role of devising and interpreting the future. It must read the signs of the future in the present and assign to the future an organic identity and a feasibility structured in political-social strategies and *ad hominem* strategies (Cambi 2006).

In other words, there is a need to educate, to shape mindsets, consciences, and individuals in such a way that they consider their own existence as a value, a rule, a limit that the society or its mechanisms cannot breach. The first step, therefore, is to educate people to understand and valorize the human being; to teach people that every individual has a 'value in itself' and a 'value for all of us', since everyone represents a remarkable and unique individual, full of potential and importance. Obviously, in all this process, dialogue plays a fundamental role: it should not hide the tensions existing between individuals belonging to different cultures, but instead it should be built on them and by them, avoiding self-referentiality, skipping ethnocentrism, and continuously working to develop a common space.

Besides, it is necessary to educate people to recognize, embrace, and spread human rights as new vision of global co-existence and its main rule. Human rights that go beyond cultures and traditions, becoming the new common dress of global co-existence; human rights that must be defined, codified, learned, and lived; in other words human rights that must be embraced with total resolution and critical sense. Above all, these rights must be promoted through dialogue, by placing cultures one in front of the other and asking them to radically confront each other, with the aim of postulating and expanding a common concept of humanity and devising the institutions that should protect it. This concept should be diffused and become a habit in this new global culture of humanity. Another fundamental aspect is to educate people to the value of equality, tolerance, and dialogue, which are the principles that create the 'space of encounter' and that represent also the launching pad of every intercultural adventure. It is important to educate people to consider diversity as a resource that helps overcoming the limits of the self and that asks for a reevaluation of the self, the identity, and the sense of belonging. It is necessary to educate people to consider integration as a process that requires mutuality, recognition, participation, and a positive welcoming attitude that must be active, participated, and mutual.

Then, as Latouche (1992) stated, it is necessary to educate people to '*décoloniser l'imaginaire*'; to avoid every *imperium*; to get rid of all forms of bias or prejudice, limitation, closed rule or identity; and to open up instead to reevaluation, de-construction, re-interpretation and demystification. Only in this way, it will be possible to enter in an open democracy characterized by encounter, dialogue, and shared built integration.

This proximity and reciprocity among individuals gives naturally birth to dialogue, which requires the ability to listen. This ability promotes accordance, understanding, and sharing among thinking and speaking individuals that during this process associate with each other. Dialogue therefore means listening, understanding, and engaging in a mutual recognition of being individuals and faces. This means that, in a space where differences meet, the encounter will truly happen only in presence of four fundamental components: confrontation, deconstruction, dialogue, and understanding.

Confrontation means standing one in front of the other and activating, in particular, the listening skill. Deconstruction instead means to take an attitude that allows getting rid of prejudices and of cognitive, ethical, or religious rigidities. Then, there is dialogue, which requires listening and the need to give a face to the individual we are talking with, to see him/her *in primis* as a person, before seeing him/her as someone with beliefs and habits. All this, on the one hand, promotes understanding, which allows for full recognition and mutual respect; while on the other hand, it opens the 'space of encounter' to a new dimension. A new playing field that fosters coexistence and recognition, and which must be cultivated as the frontline of a new cultural model, where the values of humanity and democracy consider the multicultural and intercultural inputs in a more critical and open way.

Such an intense dialogue becomes therefore the crucial model of the multicultural society in which we live, characterized by the strong need of understanding, reciprocity, and mutual recognition which are required to organize the 'space of encounter'. A space where cultures can find their place and at the same time build it, occupying and considering it as their main task.

The 'space of encounter' is therefore the fruit of the mutual dialogical tension that listening activates, which prepares the individual to hear the ideas of the other and understand their roots, creating spaces of common understanding and common *ethos* of communication and existence, which in its turn creates a real democratic community that has the ability to give birth to values of justice, solidarity, and shared accountability.

It results clear that the identification of dialogue as the key technique of the 'space of encounter' and its promotion as an open, critical, and self-critical process, leads to the idea and the implementation of a global citizenship of individuals, ethnic groups, and cultures that thrives on solidarity, irenic values, human rights, and laicity.

The complex blueprint of interculturalism that has been outlined in the previous paragraphs needs to be reviewed and developed with perseverance and vision, with audacity and resolution, because it is still *in nuce* and *in fieri* and, therefore, it requires to be accompanied in its theoretical development and in the establishment of a categorial and cognitive framework that animates it in the institutional, historical, and political project that it entails.

The 'space of encounter' is therefore a challenging space, which is and always will be the support mould used for building the multicultural society in which we live and that will have to become more intercultural; with the aim of developing, without domination purposes, a global model adapted to the age of globalization, a phenomenon that seems to be completely irreversible.

Obviously, this will be possible only through education, which is characterized by tensions and combinations between theory and practice, between planning and implementation, between the need of facing an issue and opening up to the other: an open process always *in itinere*.

The aim of education must therefore be to educate and train global human beings, global citizens that can reach this status only through dialogue and openness, by avoiding all forms of closure while keeping their own identity and embracing the ethical, dialogical, collaborative, and pluralistic principle of democracy. According to Franco Cambi, this is a true necessity in order 'to live without ideas deriving from colonialism, racism and imperialism in the geographical, demographic, political, plural, and polymorphic space represented by today's and tomorrow's world' (Cambi 2006, p. 75). A world that, after all, represents also the space that we have and we will have to occupy more and more in the future, with great respect for that universe of values ruled by the guiding and inspiring principle of unity-diversity; hinged on the square-shaped structure composed by tolerance, dialogue, integration, and rights that leads to the recognition of democracy as value.

Critical Engagement through Dialogue:
Freirean Notion of Conscientization

Considering the aspects mentioned in the previous pages, EFL classrooms are to be considered the educational space and pedagogical collection of a pluralistic philosophy that defines the teleological horizon of education, which consists in rediscovering an anthropological vision based on the undying respect of the individual. In other words, the educational process should be a 'humanization practice' that promotes the 'conscientization' of the subjects involved in order to develop their ability to overcome all forms of oppression, subjugation, and discrimination, by leading them on the path of 'humanization'. This kind of 'problem-posing education', a term coined by Paulo Freire, is based on the theory of dialogical action. According to Freire, dialogical action allows the 'oppressed' to become aware of their condition of mental subjugation. It empowers them and helps them free themselves of the 'false myths' created by the leading class and reject the fatalism that they used to justify their condition of outcasts (Freire 2005).

The practice of this 'pedagogical credo' in EFL classrooms helps in conveying the idea that English is not anymore the 'language of the empire' which tries, through subtle and hidden strategies of democratic teaching-learning processes, to label things as different or belonging to the 'Other' by manipulating ideas and identities in order to mortify the masses and their culture. Instead, English becomes the language of interculturalism that embraces common spaces where difference and its value are respected. Hence, it is considered a language that promotes a pedagogical paradigm of critical reflection about cultural pluralism, which must be enhanced and turned into a resource and growth opportunity for the values of peace, justice, equality, legality, human rights, and solidarity. Considering this aim, the concept of 'problem-posing education' proposed by Paulo Freire highlights its topicality and value. It is indeed a type of practice that gives birth to a process which is fruit of the use of a new *forma mentis*. According to the Brazilian educator, it is *'praxis'*, in other words a simultaneous reflection and action that gives birth to a *'habitus'* and a *'habitat'* of dialogue, confrontation and mutual understanding. This creates the *'forma mentis'* and the principles-values of the individual, with the aim of building a society democratically open and ready to take charge of the responsibility of community life, asking at the same time for the concrete involvement of the individual in a dimension of solidarity and respect for the Other.

According to Freire, this type of education is based on dialogue. As a matter of fact, the value and topicality of this pedagogical paradigm is fully understandable by focusing on the 'essence of dialogue', which for the South-American educator must be considered the basis of education. In *Pedagogy of the Oppressed*, Freire affirms:

> as we attempt to analyze dialogue as a human phenomenon, we discover something which is the essence of dialogue itself: the word. But the word is more than just an instrument which makes dialogue possible; accordingly, we must seek its constitutive elements. Within the word we find two dimensions, reflection and action, in such radical interaction that if one is sacrificed—even in part—the other immediately suffers. There is no true word that is not at the same time a praxis. Thus, to speak a true word is to transform the world. An unauthentic word, one which is unable to transform reality, results when dichotomy is imposed upon its constitutive elements. When a word is deprived of its dimension of action, reflection automatically suffers as well; and the word is changed into idle chatter, into *verbalism*, into an alienated and alienating 'blah' (Freire 2005: 87).

According to the Brazilian educator, dialogue is an existential necessity and the way that human beings must follow to achieve significance as human beings. It is the encounter in which the 'reflection' and 'action' of individuals combine, as they are addressed to the world which has to be transformed and humanized. According to Freire, since dialogue is an act of creation, it must necessarily take place through love, humility, faith, hope, and critical thinking.

In his *Pedagogy of the Oppressed*, the South-American educator explains that 'love' is the foundation of dialogue and commitment to others. He affirms that dialogue cannot exist in the absence of a profound love for the world and for people, since the naming of the world, which is an act of creation and re-creation, is not possible if it is not caused by love. Besides, he notices that dialogue cannot exist without 'humility', because dialogue is the encounter of those committed to the common task of creating and re-creating together, and it is broken if one of its parties lack in humility. Freire considers also people who believes in the existence of an elite and a second-rate group and affirms that people lacking humility or who have lost it do not have that 'human authenticity' which is required to get in touch with the '*Other*'. Freire explains also that dialogue cannot exist in the absence of an intense 'faith' in human beings. Faith in their power to make and remake; faith in their vocation to be more fully human, which is not the privilege of any man, but the birthright of all. According to Freire, dialogue cannot exist without 'hope', which is rooted in 'men's incompletion' and their 'dehuman- ization'. These are the reasons why it is useful to fuel hope, because it leads to the incessant pursuit of the humanity denied by injustice. Finally, dialogue cannot exist unless individuals engage in true thinking, 'critical thinking', which perceives reality as a process still in the making, where the presence of each individual is not seen as a massive presence that must adapt, but an active element and player in a field that takes shape as the individual acts upon it (Freire 2005). Therefore, in the words of Carlo Nanni, the pedagogic paradigm of the South-American educator owns a value and topicality that strongly affects also EFL classrooms:

> it assumes an essential ethical and ontological value thanks to its role of «ethical charge» that requires strictness, critical sense and moral honesty. An 'ethical charge' that strengthen the commitment and effort for the search of new information, perspectives and functional methods that have the aim of developing education projects with a high human and democratic dimension, on the basis of everything that is ontological in the human reality and existence. In particular, it is a provoca- tion that asks to go beyond today's limits, to look for new ways and unprecedented action possibilities, to give voice to those excluded or alienated from a society that has decided to proclaim itself a democracy, while it is still characterized by high levels of exclusion, social and cultural discrimination (Nanni 2002:100-01).

Critical Engagement Through Encounter: The Basis of Interculturalism

In this unique multicultural framework, the 'space of encounter' acquires a pivotal role. A thorough analysis of its profile, with the aim of stripping it down to its bare components, becomes therefore crucial.

The first device of the 'space of encounter' is the metaphoric structure of 'the view from afar', identified by Lévi-Strauss. This device is particularly useful to get in touch, know and understand 'other' cultures. It makes it possible to overcome the absoluteness, exclusivity, and defense of one's own culture. This mental structure, typical of anthropologists, is hinged on the need that everyone must deconstruct one's own self, with the aim of overstepping the borders of one's own culture and its prejudices. This must be done in order to venture in a new dialogical identity that is ready to undertake an encounter-listening-dialogue process with the identity of the 'Other' and that will allow for a complete ideographical understanding of its uniqueness and individuality.

This point of view puts things in a highly constructive perspective, because it identifies the value of difference and otherness and it gives a new way of understanding the humanity to which we all belong. A humanity that is not only made up by identity traits that are universal or general, but also by experiences, unique characteristics, and faces; besides traditions and concrete stories.

The second device of the 'space of encounter' is 'otherness'. Otherness represents a challenge, a simultaneous unsettlement and integration process that openly defies the anthropologic hierarchies of the individual, with the twofold ambition of frightening and at the same time promoting, in the 'space of encounter' that exists in every individual, confrontation, self-criticism, and the ability to re-evaluate and create a new ranking of values. Otherness brings other values, life-styles, and types of social life into the identity and this creates a 'rupture from' and a 'bond to' difference that enhances its value and makes it an alternative to our convictions.

Therefore, the discovery and recognition of otherness as value and target in this space requires the rejection of all forms of ethnocentrism and monoculturalism, accompanied by the will of taking up the challenge and opening up to other cultural models and hierarchies of values. This process leads to a rapprochement to difference and, at the same time, it helps starting a review of one's own identity, which gets enriched and strengthened by the points of view, values, and principles of the other.

Another useful device to create and protect the 'space of encounter' is 'deconstruction', which is a critical practice based not only on tolerance, but especially on the mutual exchange that takes place between two interlocutors that, through their confrontation, dialogue, and interaction, listen to each other, recognize the main components of each other's identity and unveil all manifestations of bias or prejudice. Successfully using this device, hence, means to open up one's own identity to difference, to accept the existence of difference and to be willing to meet it, whatever nature or look it might have.

Clearly, such a deconstructionist attitude is a challenging practice that goes very deep and even unsettles one's own convictions. It delegitimizes all logics of domination that might become rule or reference point. It asks those with the strongest identity and who belong to the dominant culture to commit themselves to a deep self-critical practice that might put their own identity into a brand new perspective (Cambi 2006, pp. 19-24).

Identity and Difference as Building Blocks of the Encounter

Normally, identity and difference are concepts ranked in hierarchical order: the greatest importance is given to the former; while the latter is considered an annoying factor, something that should be controlled or even deleted. Nevertheless, luckily, today's societies are trying to go beyond these guidelines. Differences are seen indeed as legit and they are given the possibility to spread around, while identities have become more complex, nuanced, and locally bounded. In this way, a need for a cultural and socio-political integration arises and it leads to a dialectic balancing act that redefines and combines these two categories. This leads to the creation of a new landscape: the 'space of encounter'. This space promotes a culture of pluralism based on universally recognized common rights that generate a mutual understanding founded on the respect of difference (Cambi 2006).

The 'space of encounter' is an intercultural place (Callari Galli 1996), made up and regulated by an interculturalism that goes beyond multiculturalism and creates a *habitus* and a *habitat* of dialogue, debate, and mutual understanding. According to Franco Cambi (2006), it is a space characterized simultaneously by a high level of complexity and tension. Its complexity is due to the fact that it is a space that features plural and asymmetric cultural models regarding their identities and roles; while its high level of tension is due to the fact that the encounter with differences and dissimilarities originates a sense of disorientation and identity crisis requiring deconstructions. This 'space of encounter' is therefore a space where it is possible to find plural identities that occupy it on a physical level and define it on a mental level. It represents therefore both a physical and inner space and, because of its nature, it is highly dynamic and always in the making.

For these reasons, the 'space of encounter' has become a pivotal and urgent task for today's society, since it teaches a vision of cultures installed in a space of encounter and dialogue, where dialogue acquires a functional and regulatory role that leads to the development (and not the disappearance) of a sense of belonging. Besides, it promotes mutual recognition and, therefore, the beginning of a new stage of redefinition.

Conclusion

The dialogical-intercultural approach described in the previous pages might seem as a new and disrupting device, nevertheless it is also necessary and full of potential, since it is very useful in order to deconstruct and reorient the practice of education and the theory of pedagogy with the aim of fully considering the thousand facets of diversity existing in the world and that represent the main asset of mankind.

Considering the fact that our future will become more interethnic and globalized, making the world a place where identities will intertwine with difference and difference will fuel identities in a continuous dialectic interplay, it is crucial for education to become a tool to avoid getting stuck in front of barriers linked to ideas of a single way of thinking or monoculture; and instead learn how to identify and respect the dignity of the *Other*, and promote an improvement and enrichment of each and everyone's humanity through a series of continuous interactions that involve and held individuals accountable in the eyes of themselves, the others, and the entire world. Hence, the need of a pedagogical responsibility which

> falls on those who are interested in the future of education and pedagogy, particularly those who believe that there is still place for a commitment to fair social justice, against all forms of political domination or cultural discrimination or economic exploitation or political subjection. Considering all these problems and issues, Freire's pedagogy can help in overcoming all forms of historical fatalism and pessimistic passivity. His pedagogy therefore could bring about a committed kind of hope, which respects the personal limits and the «dialoguing» respect for differences. It could spur the wish to leave behind the interior mutism and the

one-size-fits-all and mass-media standardization approach, allowing students to rediscover their ability to critically interpret reality and commit to their world and common destiny (Nanni 2003: 37).

Obviously, this will be possible only if we reject the idea of 'cultural self-sufficiency' and we start asking ourselves the questions that Freire highlighted in his book, *Pedagogy of the Oppressed*:

> How can I dialogue if I always project ignorance onto others and never perceive my own? How can I dialogue if I regard myself as a case apart from others—mere "its" in whom I cannot recognize other "I"s? How can I dialogue if I consider myself a member of the in-group of "pure" men, the owners of truth and knowledge, for whom all non-members are "these people" or "the great unwashed"? How can I dialogue if I start from the premise that naming the world is the task of an elite and that the presence of the people in history is a sign of deterioration, thus to be avoided? How can I dialogue if I am closed to—and even offended by—the contribution of others? How can I dialogue if I am afraid of being displaced, the mere possibility causing me torment and weakness? (Freire 2005: 90).

Probably, at least once in our lives, we have felt like we were conditioned by some particular genetic, cultural, social factors. Yet, this fact should make us understand that we might be conditioned, but not determined, and that history is a time filled with possibilities and not inexorably determined, and that the future is problematic and not already decided (Freire 2001).

For these reasons, as Freire highlights often in *Pedagogy of Freedom,* the practice of education must take strength from the belief that it is worth fighting against all hinders that might hamper the individual-student from becoming 'more fully human', since the 'what-to-do of the teacher' is a practice addressed to people who might be incomplete, curious, smart; people who might know, but who might also ignore; people who cannot live without ethics and therefore have learned contradictorily how to transgress it. As Freire states, what helps us in holding fast to this belief is the fact that history is a time filled with possibilities and not something that is inexorably determined.

Dr. Domenica Maviglia
Department of Cognitive Science, Education, and Cultural Studies
University of Messina

References

Abou, S. (1995). *Culture e diritti dell'uomo*. Turin: Sei.

Allport, G. (1973). *La natura del pregiudizio*. Florence: La Nuova Italia.

Baslev, A. N., & Rorty, R. (2001). *Noi e loro. Dialogo sulla diversità culturale*. Milan: Il Saggiatore.

Bauman, Z. (2003). *L'enigma multiculturale*. Bologna: Il Mulino.

Benhabib, S. (2005). *La rivendicazione dell'identità culturali*. Bologna: Il Mulino.

Buber, M. (1954). *Il Principio dialogico*. Milan: Ed. di Comunità, 1958.

Callari Galli, M. (1996). *Lo spazio dell'incontro*. Rome: Meltemi.

Cambi, F. (1987). *La sfida della differenza*. Bologna: Clueb.

Cambi, F. (2001). *Intercultura. Fondamenti pedagogici*. Rome: Carocci.

Cambi, F. (2006). *Incontro e dialogo. Prospettive della pedagogia interculturale*. Rome: Carocci.

Cannarozzo Rossi, G. (2007). *Analisi di pedagogia interculturale*. Soveria Mannelli: Rubbettino.

Colicchi, E. (2009). *Per una pedagogia critica*. Rome: Carocci.

Dal Fiume, G. (2000). *Educare alla differenza. La dimensione interculturale nell'educazione degli adulti*. Bologna: Emi.

Dal Lago, A. (1999). *Non-persone: l'esclusione dei migranti in una società globale*. Milan: Feltrinelli.

Delors, J. (1997). *Nell'educazione un tesoro*. Rome: Armando.

Elster, J. (Ed.). (1991). *L'io multiplo*. Milan: Feltrinelli.

Fabbri, L., & Rossi, B. (2003). *La costruzione della competenza interculturale*. Milan: Guerini.

Fanon, F. (1965). *Il negro e l'altro*. Milan: Il Saggiatore.

Fanon, F. (1996). *Pelle nera maschere bianche*. Milan: Marco Tropea Editore.

Freire, P. (2001). *Pedagogy of freedom. Ethics, democracy, and civic courage*. Maryland: Rowman & Littlefield.

Freire, P. (2005). *Pedagogy of the oppressed*. New York: The Continuum International Publishing Group.

Freire, P., & Macedo, D. (2008). *Cultura, lingua, razza. Un dialogo*. Udine: Forum.

Geertz, C. (1987). *Interpretazione di culture*. Bologna: Il Mulino.

Ghezzi, M. (1996). *Il rispetto dell'altro*. Rome: La Nuova Italia.

Giusti, M. (2005). *Pedagogia interculturale. Teorie, metodologia, laboratori*. Rome: Laterza.

Gobbo, F. (2000). *Pedagogia interculturale. Il progetto educativo nelle società complesse*. Rome: Carocci.

Grégoire, H. (2007). *La nobiltà della pelle*. Milan: Medusa Edizioni.

Hannerz, U. (2001). *La diversità culturale*. Bologna: Il Mulino, Intersezioni.

Jonas, H. (1990). *Il principio di responsabilità*. Turin: Einaudi.

Kincheloe, J. L. (2008). *Critical Pedagogy*. New York: Peter Lang.

Kymlicka, W. (1997). *Le sfide del multiculturalismo*. Bologna: Il Mulino.

Latouche, S. (1992). *L'occidentalizzazione del mondo*. Turin: Bollati Boringhieri.

Lévinas, E. (1985). *L'umanesimo dell'altro uomo*. Genoa: Il Melangolo.

Licciardi, I. (2003). *Intercultura e itinerari dell'educazione. Ricerche pedagogiche sul dialogo*. Milan: Franco Angeli.

Lyotard, J. F. (1981). *La condizione postmoderna*. Milan: Feltrinelli.

Mantegazza, R. (2003). *Pedagogia della resistenza. Tracce utopiche per educare a resistere*. Troina: Città Aperta.

Mclaren, P. (1998). *Multiculturalismo revolucionario*. Madrid: Siglo XXI.

Nanni, A. (2001). *Decostruzione e interculturalità*. Bologna: Il Mulino.

Nanni, C. (2002). *Utopia/sogno, scienza/realtà: per una ricezione italiana di Paulo Freire, oggi*. In Telleri, F. (Ed.) (2002). *Il metodo di Paulo Freire. Nuove tecnologie e sviluppo sostenibile*. Bologna: Clueb, pp. 100-101.

Pinto Minerva, F. (2002). *L'intercultura*. Rome-Bari: Laterza.

Portera, A. (2013). *Manuale di pedagogia interculturale*. Rome-Bari: Laterza.

Portera, A. & Grant, C. (Eds.). (2011). *Intercultural and multicultural education. Enhancing global interconnectedness.* New York: Routledge.

Ricoeur, P. (1993). *Sé come un altro.* Milan: Jaca Book.

Sayad, A. (2008). *L'immigrazione o i paradossi dell'alterità. L'illusione del provvisorio.* Verona: Ombre corte.

Sen, A. K. (2000). *La diseguaglianza. Un riesame critico.* Bologna: Il Mulino.

Sen, A. K. (2005). *La democrazia degli altri. Perché la libertà non è un'invenzione dell'Occidente?* Milan: Mondadori.

Sen, A. K. (2008). *Identità e violenza.* Rome-Bari: Laterza.

Steinberg, S. R. (2009). *Diversity and multiculturalism: A reader.* New York: Peter Lang.

Sundermeier, T. (1999). *Comprendere lo straniero. Una ermeneutica interculturale.* Brescia: Queriniana.

Tognon, G. (1987). *Discorso sulla dignità dell'uomo.* Brescia: La Scuola.

Touraine, A. (1997). *Eguaglianza e diversità, i nuovi compiti della democrazia.* Rome-Bari: Laterza.

Wallnöfer, G. (2000). *Pedagogia interculturale.* Milan: Bruno Mondadori.

Wieviorka, M. (2002). *La differenza culturale.* Rome: Editori Laterza.

Wieviorka, M. (2007). *L'inquietudine delle differenze.* Milan: Bruno Mondadori.

Xodo, C. (2001). *L'occhio del cuore. Pedagogia della competenza etica.* Brescia: La Scuola.

Zani, G. (2002). *Pedagogia interculturale. La convivenza possibile.* Brescia: La Scuola.

Chapter Three

The Business of Validity, Reliability and Authentic Need

Arts-based Approaches to Researching Practice

TARQUAM MCKENNA

All qualitative research, which is by definition the investigation of ideas, life features and phenomena surrounding issues that occur in natural settings, must align itself with notions of *quality* and especially *equality*. The qualitative research process that we will begin to explore here attempts to review the purposes for and reasons behind people's particular modes of engagement with the world. Qualitative research is that place where the re-searcher interprets and inquires of phenomena in terms of the meanings that the people with whom she or he engages bring to their world (Denzin 1994). It has at its ontological core an understanding that it is an appropriate method for discerning the multifaceted significances that the subject of the research attributes to the topic being investigated. So qualitative inquiry,[1] as an interpretive methodology, entails and emphasizes a naturalistic approach. Denzin and Lincoln (1994) define qualitative research as being:

> [m]ultimethod in focus, involving an interpretive, naturalistic approach to its subject matter. This means that qualitative researchers study things in their natural settings, attempting to make sense of our interpret phenomena in terms of the meanings people bring to them. Qualitative research involves the studied use and collection of a variety of empirical materials—case study, personal experience, introspective,

---

[1]   I will use the terms 'qualitative inquiry' and 'qualitative research' interchangeably throughout this chapter.

M. Vicars et al. (eds.), *The Praxis of English Language Teaching and Learning (PELT)*, 39–54.

life story, interview, observational, historical, interactional, and visual texts—that describe routine and problematic moments and meaning in individuals' lives.

The multifaceted nature of life itself means that there are a myriad of ways in which an analysis of 'life-worlds' can unfold. In this chapter, however, we shall emphasize the importance of *emancipatory practice* and *art* as vehicles for change.

Another leading scholar in the field John Creswell's definition of qualitative research—though a few years later (1997) emphasizes its social aspects. He noted that:

Qualitative research is an *inquiry* process of understanding based on distinct methodological traditions of inquiry that explore a social or human problem. The researcher builds a complex, holistic picture, analyzes words, reports detailed views of informants, and conducts the study in a natural setting.

The researcher then addresses the 'field' or 'matter' under study and, in so doing, gives priority to how the data contributes to the critical research questions so as to deepen the sense of understanding around the prevailing information.

The Praxis of English Language Teaching and Learning

It Is So Diffuse—What Really Matters?

Within the fields of language studies, critical literacy and education generally, the evidence gained from qualitative research is wide-ranging and diffuse in nature. Qualitative research necessarily encompasses a range of beliefs, research designs and specific practices and findings, which will be examined as this chapter unfolds. The reader will be introduced to, and it is hoped, become familiar with a range of varied techniques for data collection. These include in-depth qualitative interviews; participant and non-participant observation; focus groups; document analyses; and a number of other methods.

Before reaching the point of learning more about the main ways of doing the work, we need to ask of ourselves, as researchers, two crucial questions that lie at the core of critical education and critical pedagogy: *Why do research in education?* and *What is praxis?* In its *Qualitative Research in Educational Planning* series of publications, the international agency UNESCO (Postlethwaite, 2005, p. 29) asks us to pay attention to the political activity of education with the aim of always improving education and schooling in order to redress emergent 'shortcomings'.

> Each system of education has its political goals, its general educational goals, and its specific educational objectives. For example, some political goals stress equality of opportunity, others stress quality of education, and many stress both.
>
> In every system of education changes are made by educational planners with the aim of improving the quality of education. These changes can include a revised curriculum, new methods of teacher training, increasing the amount of provisions to schools, changing the structure from a selective to a comprehensive system, reducing class size and many other changes. In some cases, innovations need to be tried out to identify their likely shortcomings, effects, and side effects before they are implemented. In other cases, student achievement over time in one or more subjects needs to be monitored, or where there are optional subjects the percentage of a grade or age group selecting such subjects needs to be known. Or, the attitudes and perceptions of students need to be assessed.

This is the purpose of this chapter—to examine the motivations underlying the critical and emancipatory capacities of research. Given the above notation and the intentions it assumes, how do we critically revise the world of the school so as to place stress on quality and equality? These two matters are at the heart of critical inquiry. The revision of curricula, the evaluation of teacher preparation, the provision of equal resources to schools and the undertaking of innovative methods to bring about an enhanced quality of education must reflect these aspects in our research efforts. The range of data types that critical inquiry that can and does use are as diverse as the methodologies, philosophies and theories that underlie the field of critical research (or critical inquiry), but it is these two key words—'quality' and 'equality'—that must shape all research practice.

The eminent Australian researchers Allan Luke and Karen Dooley (2011) highlight the transformative power of language learning and we sense from their ideas that equity and quality are noted as central themes that contribute to change. They use the term 'critical literacy' to connote how language is used as a cultural, social and political practice to address 'marginalized' people:

Critical literacy is the use of texts to analyse and transform relations of cultural, social and political power. It is part of a longstanding normative educational project to address social, economic and cultural injustice and inequality. It aims towards the equitable development and acquisition of language and literacy by historically marginalized communities and students, and towards the use of texts in a range of communications media to analyse, critique, represent and alter inequitable knowledge structures and social relations of school and society.

This definition holds to the pioneering principles espoused by one of the leaders in critical pedagogy, Paolo Freire (1993, 1994), whose legacy in these matters stretches back nearly half a century. For Freire, teaching and learning (that is, pedagogy) are occasions for the addressing of, relating to and dealing with the structures and affairs of society through its governmental, political and cultural powers by recognising the essential material and social consequences and possibilities for learners and their communities. By building upon the theoretical positions of critical pedagogy (see McKenna & Cacciattolo, 2012) and on the work of Freire in particular, I can confidently assert that there is a greater likelihood for the development in individuals of a yearning for learning for its own sake *when the motivation for research is apparent* and that such motivation is central to *finding meaningful moments in the research*. There can be little doubt that this *is best realized when the researched community works in collaboration with the researcher*. The skillful, respectful and motivating researcher can *re*-create and *re*-invent the lived world alongside the learner-as-researcher. As I have noted elsewhere (McKenna & Cacciattolo, 2012, p. 60) the teacher or researcher

must not only recreate what is already apparent in the space of their teaching. Through 'action and reflection-on-action' (Schon, 1995), the student and teacher alike can have high aspirations as they co-create, collaborate and re-invent politically rich teaching and learning moments where private, public and professional Englishes intersect. Opportunities for strengthening notions of agency, civics and respectful citizenship can only emerge when students and teachers alike are actively involved in questioning, probing and critically evaluating the construction of learner identities and their place in the society in which they live.

Again, the emphasis here is on how equitable and available learning is to the students who might otherwise have been least advantaged (Connell, 1993). This is captured by Freire (1993, p. 83) who speaks of the need to educate and research in order to promote a criticality that is void of passivity and numbness.

> In problem-posing education, people develop their power to perceive critically the way they exist in the world with which and in which they find themselves; they come to see the world not as a static reality, but as a reality in process, in transformation. Although the dialectical relations of women and men with the world exist independently of how these relations are perceived (or whether or not they are perceived at all), it is also true that the form of action they adopt is to a large extent a function of how they perceive themselves in the world. Hence, the teacher-student and the students-teachers reflect simultaneously on themselves and the world without dichotomizing this reflection from action, and thus establish an authentic form of thought and action.

Research is 'critical' when it has significance for both the researcher and the researched. That is, both senses of the word should be apparent in the motivations behind and exercise of research: it should be 'critical' in that it seeks to question and discern, but also in that it should *matter*. The research itself should be decisive, vital and address important matters crucial to the heart of the field of inquiry. The ideal for inquiry is that the research is in and of itself so vital that it is indispensable. And so any research that we call critical inquiry and that is based on critical pedagogy is to be designed to address questions around the notions of freedom, of equality and, ultimately, of liberation. Teachers of languages other than English (and the assumption is that this group forms the core readership of a text such as this) know that reading, writing and work with the printed text and other forms of language are always culturally specific. And often the English language (be it American, British, Australian or Canadian English) is covertly and even tacitly privileged. When learning English through the lens of critical inquiry there is always a need to realize that all language is best taught within a context that is meaningful for the learner. Pedagogical research should ideally address and attempt to redress the sometimes tacit, sometimes explicit, 'colonization' of the cultural context in which English is being taught.

UNESCO captures this intention of critical inquiry when it asks the reader of its report, *Educational Research: Some Basic Concepts and Terminology* (Postlethwaite, 2005) to undertake an exercise. (This is actually something that any individual could and, I would say, should undertake.) The exercise takes the form of an exploration that seeks to prioritize those areas of need for a particular country's education system. That is, to 'operationalize' research as a process in order to consider how the education system in that country performs (or does not perform).

The examination occurs through a series of practices that address specific phenomena. So, in an Australian context it might be as succinct as exploring how five general aims taken from a small policy publication—in this case, *Planning for Successful Schooling*, which was prepared by the Ministry of Education in the State of Victoria during 1990—have been actualized 25 years on. The UNESCO authors' aim at the imposition of general operational principles that have critical empowerment at their core to specific phenomena, so, paraphrasing UNESCO (Postlethwaite, 2005, p. 49), we would ask how Victorian schools now provide opportunities to:

1. Expand educational *opportunities* for all students?

2. Encourage *excellence in all areas of learning* and to assist *all students* to develop their full potential?

3. *Strengthen community* participation in and satisfaction with the state school system?

4. *Develop and improve the skills, potential and performance* of school principals, teachers, and administrative and support staff?

5. *Manage and control financial and physical resources* in ways, which maximize educational benefits for *all students*?

These five questions (with my italics added) are admittedly very broad, but each encapsulates those senses of equality, equity and quality of opportunity for learning as the goal for inquiry, that the researcher using the lens of critical pedagogy must undertake. The phenomena to be examined are, respectively, 'opportunities' 'excellence in all learning areas' 'assistance with development of full potential, 'strengthening community participation' and the consideration of satisfaction and improvement in the 'performance' of schools. And these issues are framed within their relevance to 'all students' as well as to their whole school communities. Financial and physical resources form the basis of the final and pivotal question to be deliberated upon. Still, it is control over the school that lies at the centre of the shared quest as the UNESCO exercise below interrogates.

EXERCISE 1 (INDIVIDUAL WORK)

Select one of the five general aims above that you believe would probably receive a high priority in your country. For that general aim write five specific research questions. For each of these five research questions, prepare several operationalized research aims that focus on the performance of the education system in meeting these aims. Then, write down a broad outline of the sequence of activities that would need to be undertaken in order to assess the system's performance with respect to these aims.

How does the researcher then examine the knowledge produced by asking such a complex range of questions that impact of the interrogation of the field of inquiry whether in Australia or elsewhere in the world? Could these questions be asked in a worldwide context and in a way that would evoke new knowledge that will assist actions leading to emancipation? Ideally the answer to this essential question rests upon the fundamental work that is chosen by and with the community under study. In the Australian Council for Educational Research's Radford Memorial Lecture of 1987, New Zealand's former Minister of Education, Dr. Clarence Beeby (in Postlethwaite, 2005, p. 11), was obviously aware of this vital part of any policymaking process and launched a call to action to researchers that we would do well to remember.

> I have suggested areas of research that seem to me to be of special importance. But not once have I asked a specific question to which I want an answer… I know enough about research to be aware that the formulation of the proper question may take as much skill and professional insight as the finding of an answer to it, and it may be a skill in which the administrator is not adept. So, the research workers must be involved in the asking of the questions, and must be prepared, in turn, to play a necessary, but secondary, part devising the policies that may follow from the research, where their expertise is limited.

Beeby's words are as relevant today as they were a quarter of a century ago. That it must be a sense of necessity that drives our questioning. For him it is the whole community of policy makers and research workers who must be engaged in the practice of inquiry. To this I would add the essential participation of *the researched community*. It is the collective totality of collaboration that drives the validity of the research. Luke and Dolley (2011) bring the matter of collective, collaborative and transformational research to the fore by challenging us to ask only those sorts of research questions that can be viewed in terms of the transformative effect they generate in their outcomes. That is, whether and how the research can generate new knowledge (Luke and Dolley's case, literacies) that have the capacity to alter

> communities' critical analyses and action in the world and their material and social relations, individually and collectively, developmentally and longitudinally.

Qualitative research has 'validity' only inasmuch as transformative power, as much as is possible, belongs to and resides within the representatives of the community being questioned. *If the research doesn't matter to its subjects, then the research itself doesn't matter.* The purposes of any inquiry that research workers undertake, the transformative effect that it generates and the appropriateness of the processes involved, drive the extent to which any research can be seen as valid. What we do as researchers is ask questions so that data will be collected, collated, synthesise and reported *for action*.

The appropriateness of research to the phenomena investigated as summarised in the above discussion is based on principles I have articulated elsewhere (McKenna, 2012a). Researchers need to engage in reporting on and articulating the re/presentation of the lived experience of the people they study. I call this Transformative Artful Praxis and define the term as research that *sets out* to review and capture how places *are created* for learning (in schools in this instance—perhaps for learners of English as speakers of other languages) as experiential practice for all people whom the researcher encounters. The principle that I espouse and note above is that research should, indeed must, always be approached as an *opportunity for collaborative inquiry* and connectivity-through-engagement aimed at building respectful and collective knowing and knowledge. The making of meaning of the life-worlds of any 'researched' community or individual requires that the principles of respect and collective ownership of the research occur. The researcher needs to engage in a process of reflective practice, which consists of a personal and critical interrogation of their own acculturated *and innate assumptions and beliefs* concerning the community of researched people. And I hold that we need to re/create stories and re/use personal narratives to explore notions of the community, identity and research question. Unlike quantitative inquiry qualitative inquiry can become an occasion in which we are permitted to 'speak' our own truths and so it becomes, in some sense, a form of relational knowledge creation.

The story-telling practice that I advocate holds at its essence the belief that psychosocial wellness dwells at the core of all identity. This means that many times the researcher, the researched and the question will generate the need to explore *tensions and anomalies* whilst simultaneously generating opportunities for the integration of the individual and collective identities being 'questioned'. The diagram on the following page illustrates the various components of this approach.

The Slice-of-Life Approach

As researchers we are obliged to consider that just as judgments of the *veracity* of Art works lie beyond the ken of postmodern critiques concerning absolute and 'documentary' truths (McKenna, 1999), so too, does Artful practice, and the praxis of Artful research explore the tensions and anomalies that are at the heart of evocative inquiry. Through the use of artworks we can, by building on a quality of 'relatedness' move beyond a mere development of a 'sociology of life' or the slice-of-life approach towards a deeper place of expression using the field of Art-making. In encouraging researchers to use anti-foundationalist approaches to Art forms to inform a deliberate use of Artful practice to undergird their research, I am encouraging colleagues to yearn for the unveiling of a depth of meaning by bringing that which is unique into the collective ever-unfolding story that their data reveals. This method of researching is not concerned with recognizing truths or with 'comprehending' existence in some absolute and limiting way, but is much more holistic. It is a call to return to a space where artists-as-researchers and

Artful Praxis in Relation to Other Ways of 'Researching' Our Meaning

Research perspective	Experimental	Naturalistic	Transformative	Artful Praxis
Application	Comprehension	Interpretation	Learning about self and others	Liberation through aesthetics and Art as practice and experiences
Means of expression	Prediction	Description	Collaboration	Connectivity through the ritual use of each Arts practice
Intention	Add credence	Uncover theories of meaning	Interrogate assumptions & beliefs	Creating the story using Art – to break the silences. To know our individual and collective (we-connectivity) truths. To especially make the from colonized notions of identity.
Viewpoint	The "I" is prioritied	The "I and You" are visible	The sense is "We" vulnerable	Us Community and Artists working to build respectful collective knowing.
Stance on knowledge	Fixed	Contextual	Relational	Emerging from unknown realms– unconscious material made 'conscious' in art products. Knowledge is process, co-creation and community-focused Knowledge is related to psychosocial wellness.
Procedures adopted	Test hypothesis	Multiple perspectives	Tensions & anomalies	Movement toward Integration Paratherapeutic knowing
Methodological stance	Innocent	Relative	Democratic	Social justice Equity Respect Mutuality
Pathway to understanding	Simplicity	Complexity	Reflexivity	Inter-reflexivity (exhibited as products) Intra-reflexivity (interior focused–felt as artistic 'process') Self-hood Lifeworlds

Role of research relative to schooling in our society	Cultural literacy	Cultural diversity	Morality	Critical pedagogical focused on deep knowing A 'gnosis' –new emerging ever changing Art forms and literacies with knowing of self and other in the myriad of lifeworlds through the Art form
How significance is determined	Individual makes meaning	Cooperative meanings	Collaborative meanings	Witnessing "connectivity" through arts works, community and intimacy of making a shared meaning as an audience to research
Consequences	Better or Cleaner Arguments	More complex explanations	Learning & new invitations to inquiry	Invitation to build community and co-create new ways of respectful engagements beyond those that already exist.
Product	Study	Thick description	Journey	Depth encounter with of 'otherness' as reparation of injustice.

I acknowledge the contribution made to this model of research by John Carroll, Jonathan Fox, Davina Woods and Edward Errington both in conversation and in past publications where this model has been presented in varied forms.

Table 3.1. Model of Artful Practice (McKenna & Woods, 2012)

researchers-as-artists can work together towards presenting a wholeness of understanding; it is a space already mapped out to some extent by the life-world practices of those who would seek to understand. And like any map it is a work-in-progress, a shifting, changing document (not documentary) that alters as new roads open and old avenues close, as fields become populated with new arrivals and once unassailable edifices are bulldozed to make way for progressive spaces of play and contemplation.

The ultimate unattainable goal of making wholly present the presence of those people being 'researched' on such maps cannot be overstated; its very unattainability should present as an active, welcome occasion for discussions *of social justice, equity, respect and mutuality. So the researcher needs to be a person who can use their own engagement with manifold fields of inquiry as an occasion for reflexive, self-knowing explorations of self-hood with respect to the life-worlds of everyone involved in the research in the quest to co-create ways for the respectful engagement with and building of the community to which we all belong.* In many ways it is the creation of a map which precedes the territory. The work is creative; always personal, in-depth and descriptive while at the same time cognizant of and attendant to the ever-changing societal aspects of our world.

The Practices

The terms and practice of phenomenology, ethnography, grounded theory, action research and case studies are all examined elsewhere and can be easily accessed by readers of this chapter. But as these are often vehicles which drive the researchers' perspective we should take some time to describe what is at the heART of these modes of inquiry. These ways of examining and being 'alongside' the research question all generate stories; human stories especially. They provide cumulative sets of data and 'findings' that can form the bases for heartfelt (Ellis, 1999, pp. 669-683) analysis. And ideally these 'findings' echo the voices of the community of minds as they embody the knowledge that researchers explore in their practice of the research process. And, once again, these shared stories are the 'supporting evidence' that enable transformation to occur.

The process of qualitative inquiry is intrinsically democratic in that it can engage with the community through in-depth interviews, focus group interviews, document and policy content analysis, ethnographies, evaluation of open-ended survey responses, literature reviews, audio recordings, Art-making and the employment of other information technologies. The very diversity of processes available to the researcher is one of the major strengths of qualitative research. Although there is no mandatory fixed process for approaching a qualitative research project, there are some established approaches and phases that must necessarily be taken. If we were intent on exploring opinions towards a topic, for example, the use of interviews would be anticipated; the analysis of document or policy content could occur as a program evaluation in which interview and thematic analysis accompany observation. This would then require a form of literature review to support the researcher in the illustration and accumulation of academic authority and trustworthiness. Trustworthiness of data has become familiar to us as a way to validate a qualitative methodology. It is a notion increasingly being attended to by researchers to address the normalising effect of social, psychological and cultural discourses in research practice (Dokter, 2011) and is strongly aligned with the critical emancipatory research as mentioned earlier. The trustworthiness of the data is crucial to any field of inquiry. Ellis and Bochner (2003, p. 199) use the criteria of plausibility and trustworthiness rather than of reliability and validity to situate data gathered when working with people and they remind us that the "human communication is not an object, or a discipline studying objects". The research space and the inquiry practice advocated here emphasizes that ethnographies—working with groups of people—are community-focused processes addressing human social interactions and the dynamic nature of human activity. When communicating the study of humans studying humans communicating, we are always inside what we are researching. The physical sciences tell us that the days of the uninvolved observer are past. The researcher and the researched are always personally and intimately involved in the communicative space they co-create—always using the world of reflexive praxis to address the notions of text-and-life or life-and-text—as an expression of their will to find new knowledge (McKenna & Cacciattolo, 2012). The trustworthiness required in such relationships leads us to consider ways to articulate experience whilst reflecting and reflecting on a subject or theme by accepting its connection with the psychic and emotional life of the researched group. Qualitative research is an articulation of a level of emotionality, and emotionality, subjectivity and affect all come together, I contend, through this Artful method of examining life. And this method becomes emancipatory when it offers socially transformative possibilities. Research, through its manipulation and interpretation by the researcher and the researched as they work collaboratively with their data, can present the world-as-it-is-seen and to address a coherent, collective understanding of reality, so that its findings offer a depth of insight that might not be otherwise available to the researcher.

Conclusion

This leads us back to ponder *quality* and *equality*; back to where we started. Language teaching must, of course, redress the inequities faced by the marginalized and alienated communities we encounter. It must also assume an equivalence, an *equality*—an equality of humanity and existential relevance—between the academic and the actual, between the research and the researched. And so we are compelled to wonder on and come to realize that whatever 'findings' we arrive at are always *pluralized* and dependent on the society in which the research occurs—and that communities are formed through a variety of social and culturally specific activities unique to each community, including their own self-research. How, researchers must ask themselves, in this fast-moving globalized cultural field and with the interplay of economics as the key to success, might our research be truthful? How do we live in the world we are now familiar with and yet interrupt the presumption that there is only one way to be known in order to come to know the multitude of worlds? The internationalization of curriculum alongside the new demographic and cultural conditions occurring daily needs to work towards moving beyond the privileging of native English-speaking Western societies—especially as we now are more likely to have new arrivals as migrants and refugees.

Each of us, researcher and citizen alike, needs to ask ourselves which languages we tacitly privilege in our work with language learning and how do we subvert the covert subjugation of such privileging? We need to listen to the stories that we tell each other with ears that generously and actively attend to the import of each other's narratives, rather than limiting ourselves to mere technicalities such as grammar and spelling. The democratic and inclusive *quality* of Art is just one, though an extremely effective and important way of appreciating that any research project worth doing must have as its goal the advancement of social justice for all people, everywhere. For if human research does not ultimately seek to provide the possibility that we all may lives of quality and equality, we lose our humanity.

Dr. Tarquam McKenna
College of Education
Victoria University

References

Carroll, J., Cacciattolo, M., & McKenna, T. (2012). Positive education: The use of self-study research methodology to assess its place in higher education settings. In S. Steinberg & G. Canella (Eds.) *Critical Qualitative Research (CQR) Reader* (pp. 512-523) Peter Lang: New York.

Connell, R.W. (1993). *Schools and social justice*. Leichardt, NSW: Pluto Press.

Cresswell, J. W. (1997). *Qualitative inquiry and research design: Choosing among the five traditions.* Thousand Oaks: Sage Publications.

Denzin, N. K., & Lincoln, Y. S. (1994). Introduction: Entering the field of qualitative research. In N. K. Denzin & Y. S. Lincoln (Eds.), *Handbook of qualitative research* (pp. 1-17). Thousand Oaks, CA: Sage.

Dokter, D. (2011). *Dramatherapy and destructiveness: Creating the evidence base, playing with Thanatos.* New York: Routledge.

Ellis, C. (1997). Evocative autoethnography: Writing emotionally about our lives. in W. G. Tierney & Y. S. Lincoln (Eds.) *Representation and the text: Re-framing the narrative voice* (pp. 115-139) Albany, NY: State University of New York.

Ellis, C. (1999). Heartfelt autoethnography. *Qualitative Health,* 9, (5), 669-683.

Ellis, C., & Bochner. A.P. (2003). Autoethnography, personal narrative, reflexivity: Researcher as Subject. In N.K. Denzin & Y. S. Lincoln (Eds.), *Collecting and interpreting qualitative materials, 2ⁿᵈ Ed.* (pp. 199-258). Sage Publications.

Freire, P. (1993). *Pedagogy of the oppressed.* New York: Continuum.

Freire, P. (1994). *Pedagogy of hope: Reliving pedagogy of the oppressed.* New York: Continuum.

Luke, A. & Dooley, K. (2011). Critical literacy and second language learning. In E. Hinkel (Ed.) *Handbook of Research on Second Language Teaching and Learning, Vol. 2* (pp. 856-858), New York: Routledge.

McKenna, T., & Cacciattolo, (2012). The role of CLT in teaching and learning. *Journal of Asian Critical Education JACE,* Fall 2012, (1).

McKenna, T., Cacciattolo, M., & Mahon, L. (2010). *A research evaluation of the SWIRL project: A collaborative project for indigenous community literacy and teacher education.* Department of Education, Employment and Workplace Relations. Canberra, Australia: AGPS.

McKenna, T. & Woods, D. (2012) Using psychotherapeutic arts to decolonise counselling for indigenous people. *Asia Pacific Journal of Counselling and Psychotherapy, Vol 3*(1).

McKenna, T. & Carpenter, C. (2012). Exploring. In A. Pryor, C. Carpenter, C. L. Norton, & J. Kirchner, J. (Eds.) *Emerging insights: International perspectives on adventure therapy* (pp. 270-283), Proceedings of the 5th International Adventure Therapy Conference, University of Edinburgh, Scotland. Prague, Czech Republic: European Science and Art Publishing.

McKenna, T., Woods, D., & C. Lawson (in press). Indigenous art therapy. In A. Gilroy, S. Linnell, T. McKenna, & J. Westwood (Eds.), *Art therapy: Taking a post colonial aesthetic turn.* Sydney, Australia: Bentham Books

McKenna, T (2012a). Arts education. Let's do the arts stuff on Friday afternoon—Do the arts really matter?. In T. McKenna, M. Vicars & M. Cacciattolo (Eds.), *Engaging the disengaged* (pp. 73-89). Melbourne: Cambridge University Press.

McKenna, T. (2012b) Conclusion—Purposeful, optimistic learning engagements, In T. McKenna, M. Vicars & M. Cacciattolo (Eds.), *Engaging the disengaged* (pp. 223-232). Melbourne: Cambridge University Press.

Postlethwaite, N. (2005) Educational research: some basic concepts and terminology. *Qualitative research in educational planning series.* UNESCO Publications.
    Accessed http://www.unesco.org/iiep/PDF/TR_Mods/Qu_Mod1.pdf

Schon, D. (1995). *Reflective practitioner: How professionals think in action.* Aldershot, England: Arena

Chapter Four

Ethical Considerations in Research

MARCELLE CACCIATTOLO

For beginning researchers undertaking their first major research project, can often be a time of mixed emotions. Initial meetings with supervisors or research collaborators involve addressing questions around the nature and scope of the research question, the methodological tools that will be used to collect data and the ease with which entry into the field of research is possible. The research paradigm that will be adopted is also a vital point of clarification that should be discussed during these initial scoping stages. Similarly, distinctions between methodology and methods should be understood so that the novice researcher is aware of basic concepts and terminology particular to the research process (Nyame-Asiamah & Patel, 2009; Bouma & Ling, 2004). Becoming familiar with the language of academic research is therefore an important first step when starting a scholarly investigation.

In addition to understanding the discourse of academic research, being aware of what constitutes *ethical research* is an essential part of planning for a research project. This matter of ethical research is the basis of this chapter. At all times the researcher should ensure that participants are safe from harm and are protected from unnecessary stress. This is the field of ethics.

M. Vicars et al. (eds.), *The Praxis of English Language Teaching and Learning (PELT)*, 55–73.

Unethical research that is carried out almost always leaves participants and researchers feeling vulnerable and exposed in negative ways. Unethical behaviour that is displayed by researchers can also compromise the validity and trustworthiness of data that is collected. This is especially the case if participants feel that their physical or mental well-being is threatened in some way (Orb, Eisenhauer, & Wynaden, 2001; Escobedo, Guerrero, Lujan, Ramirez, & Serrano, 2007). In order to avoid unwanted research dilemmas such as this, it is therefore important to ensure that careful planning and ethical standards are adhered to (Bouma,& Ling 2004). Good research then has at its core a commitment to ensuring that strategies for collecting data are responsible; that at all times research attends to a professional code of conduct that ensures that safety of all the participants involved.

Research that is conducted in settings where participants are non-native speakers of English can involve additional ethical reflections for researchers. Non-native speakers of English are variously categorised as speaking English as a second language (ESL), English as a foreign language (EFL) or English as an additional language (EAL). I shall use the term 'EAL' to cover all these categories. The important work of Joanna Koulouriotis (2011) draws attention to the complexities that arise when conducting research with non-native speakers of English. Cultural boundaries, translation issues, perceptions of power and authority are all 'ethical considerations inherent in and raised by ESL research' (p. 1). Koulouriotis further reiterates the point that a great proportion of research in ESL 'is conducted by teacher-researchers and/or researchers in countries where ethical concerns may not be addressed formally or by encompassing human rights legislation' (p. 1). With this in mind, this chapter examines four themes of ethical deliberations that researchers working in the field of EAL should consider. These four themes are: informed consent; deception; privacy and confidentiality and cross-cultural representation. Based on William Tierney's (1997) principle of ethnographic fiction, this chapter uses a series of 'fictional vignettes' that draw attention to the human story and the emotional distress that can emerge when research goes awry. The reader is invited to read the text as a script and to see the interactions, encounters and exchanges as these occur. Narrative is used because we often remember the 'story' and the meaning we attach to it long after the words on the pages cease to be. Our feelings and the energy of a story can also have a way of bubbling up to the surface at different times. During these times resonating stories can provide us with an emotionally charged account to fall back on when making sense of social and professional situations.

Informed Consent

Nhung is Vietnamese and lives in Ho Chi Minh City. He is an experienced teacher and thinks pretty highly of his ability to inspire and transform young people's lives. For the past ten years Nhung has taught English at a local secondary school and has favoured the use of the Communicative Language Teaching (CLT) method. Nhung's believes that the CLT method is an effective language teaching approach that provides students with opportunities to enhance their English language skills in meaningful ways. Not all of the teachers at the school share Nhung's passion for the CLT method. There are some teachers who prefer to use grammar textbooks and grammar drills when teaching English. Nhung frequently enters into debates with some of these teachers believing the grammar translation method to be disconnected to the lived experience or life-worlds of his Vietnamese students. He believes that peer-mentoring sessions need to be factored into the school calendar so that he can share his expertise with other staff members. In particular Nhung thinks that Phuong, a first year out teacher, could benefit from working with him more closely.

Nhung is enrolled in a Master of Teaching English to Speakers of Other Languages (TESOL) and is in his final year of study. He is currently completing his minor thesis and has devised his research question on the impact of using the CLT approach in improving English language proficiency.

Nhung speaks to the principal about his research project and states that he would like to work with Phuong to collect his data. He has known the principal for many years and has a strong professional relationship with him that is based on mutual respect. Nhung is therefore hopeful that the principal will be excited about the prospect of Nhung mentoring a junior colleague. The principal agrees to Nhung's research idea and commits to telling Nhung of this exciting opportunity during the day.

The lunchtime bell has rung. Phuong has just been told by the principal that she will be involved in Nhung's research project. 'You know you
are very lucky to be singled out by Nhung,' he exclaims. 'He wants to
mentor you and show you how you can improve your teaching practice.'

Phuong can't believe her luck! Out of the 50 teachers at the school,
Phuong dislikes Nhung the most. She finds him arrogant and pushy and
is irritated by his habit of butting into other people's conversations. She
is upset that her teaching appears to be seen in a negative way and feels
incredibly embarrassed by this unsolicited opportunity. Phuong is on a
one-year contract at the school and does not want to be seen to behave in
any way that might disadvantage her future employment at the school. As
a result, she chooses not to disclose her true feelings and agrees to work
with Nhung.

As seen in the case above, informed consent is a fundamental component of conducting ethical research. Informed consent can be given either
verbally or through signing a consent form. Verbal consent is often employed if a participant is illiterate or is not physically present during the
research process. Participants who decide to become involved in scientific
research should do so willingly and on a voluntary basis (Hesse-Biber &
Leavy, 2011; Locke, Acorn, & O'Neill, 2013). Prior to giving consent, individuals should be clear on the aims, methodology and potential risks they
may encounter as a result of being involved in the research. The issues of
language and communication connect here. McKay (2006, p. 28) suggests
that teachers who are working with non-English students should use a language that students are familiar with. Using the native language of students
will and does help to minimise the risk of poor communication. Effective
communication pertaining to the parameters of a research proposal helps to
ensure that students are fully aware of what is required of them should they
choose to participate. Hawkins & Emanuel (2008, p. 28) makes note of the
benefits of this kind of transparency in that it, heightens the awareness and
sensitivity of the researchers. Knowing that others know what you are doing,
and why, can be a useful way of instigating a sense of accountability that may
itself serve to reinforce ethical conduct among researchers.

As detailed above, Phuong felt pressured by the school principal to participate in Nhung's research project. Children can also feel anxious or scared when research is forced upon them. Safeguarding children from being pushed into an unwanted research encounter is fundamental to conducting ethical research.[11] Morrow and Richards (1996, p. 98) highlight that 'the biggest ethical challenge for researchers working with children is the disparities in power and status between adults and children'. With a large proportion of EAL research conducted by teacher researchers on their students, the issue of explicit and implicit power relationships is an important aspect to consider. Stocker (2012, p. 54) makes clear that teachers who are researching language contexts can 'put students' freedom of choice and speech at risk' by virtue of students feeling pressured to participate. Ethical research involving children and students should therefore consider the rights of young people so that negative feelings are minimised and avoided.

Hood, Kelley and Mayall (1996, p.118) refer to the 'risk' element of research involving children when they are viewed as 'the object of the enterprise to be studied'. This kind of standpoint can be attributed to inexperienced or naïve researchers who view children's perceptions and voices as incompetent or untrustworthy (Smith & Taylor 2000, pp. 3-4). When young people's voices are silenced or ignored, there is less likelihood that the data collected is authentic or of any real value to the research being conducted. Coercing participants like Phuong to participate in a study can also impact on the quality of data being collected. According to Mitchell (2004. p. 1430), 'the sorts of data collection that require student assent are very likely to fail to give useful data if there is any perception (let alone reality) of coercion: collecting good interview data, for example, requires students happy to elaborate on initial comments'. Creating research settings that encourage children or adults to freely give their opinions on aspects of language teaching and learning is essential to conducting effective research with favourable outcomes. On returning to the narrative, we can see how coercion is only one kind of pitfall that needs to be avoided in the process of ethical inquiry. We will look now at deception in research and how this must also be carefully considered in the conduct of respectful and collaborative research.

---

[1]   Parental/guardian consent is needed when researchers work with students who are under the age of 18 years.

Deception

Nhung's thesis submission deadline was soon approaching. He had spent two weeks observing Phuong's English language class and was pleased with the detailed field notes he had collected. The postgraduate student was at the final stage of collecting his data and this involved conducting a focus group session with ten of Phuong's students. In Nhung's estimation, giving students the opportunity to talk about their language teacher's approach would generate stronger evidence to suggest that her grammar translation approach did little to evoke innovative language teaching. Most importantly, these data findings would serve to strengthen the need to ensure that all English language teachers at the school embedded CLT strategies in their classroom practice.

The time finally came for Nhung to invite Phuong's students to participate in a focus group session. When he asked for volunteers there was complete silence in the classroom. No hands were raised; not one student expressed an interest in wanting to participate. The reason for this lack of excitement was simple. Throughout his time in the classroom, Nhung had heavily critiqued and criticised the students' level of English language proficiency in a public way. Many of the students felt embarrassed and humiliated when their mistakes were brought to the attention of their peers and Miss Phuong. These kinds of displays of their work had not been carefully explained to the parents and their children prior to consent being given. The only information they were given was that Nhung would observe the students and Miss Phuong at the back of the class and that he would run a final focus group session at the end of his study. Overall the students believed that they and their parents had been tricked into giving consent and this angered them greatly. What Nhung failed to explain were the kinds of personal, social and psychological risks that could be encountered if the students chose to participate. The research was far from Nhung's description of 'having a warm and caring intent so as to benefit of the students' English language learning'.

Phuong also felt uncomfortable with Nhung's presence in her classroom. The entire experience had left this beginning teacher feeling exposed and discombobulated. After Nhung's appraisal of her teaching mistakes, Phuong wondered whether she had the right set of skills to be able to teach English in an effective way. In his last two sessions, Nhung had insisted that he videotape Phuong while she was teaching. Filming her teaching approach was not a data collection technique that had been outlined on the consent form that she had signed. Like her students, Phuong believed that she had been deceived by Nhung and was angry that he had not been more transparent about the data collection techniques that he intended to use throughout his project.

Deception is another significant attribute that constitutes unethical research. Deception in this chapter is referred to as the 'intentional misrepresentation of facts related to the purpose, nature, or consequences of an investigation' (Drew, Hardman, & Hosp, 2008, p. 67). While there is abundant research that documents why deception may be used in research (Kimmel, Smith, & Klein, 2010; Bortolotti & Mameli, 2006; Nicks, Korn, & Mainieri, 1997), this chapter will focus on when the use of deception is problematic and outweighs the potential benefits to participants involved. Essentially, deception in research can occur in two main stages: the recruitment phase and when the research is conducted. During the recruitment phase, to misinform participants about the true nature of the investigation or to provide only selective pieces of information concerning how the study will be conducted can have adverse consequences in the long term. For both the students and Phuong, as seen in their reflections above, not being given a true and accurate account of what their involvement entailed left them feeling 'cheated' and tricked into participating. In the case of conducting ethical research, it is important that the researcher provides an honest and transparent account of all stages of the data collection process. Giving out consent forms and information sheets that clearly detail the research process helps to maintain a trusting relationship between the researcher and the participants involved in a study.

Critics argue that in circumstances where there is a loss of trust in the researcher that this almost always impacts on the quality of their relationship with their subjects (Lawson, 1997; Pierce, 2009). Drew, Hardman and Hosp (2008) make note of the fact that if participants feel deceived, they may respond in ways that can seek to 'threaten' the collection of accurate and trustworthy data. This is especially the case when participants believe that there is a hidden agenda to the study. This may result in 'responding in a manner that they think that the researcher desires, or they might try to outguess the researcher and sabotage the study' (p. 67). The participants in Nhung's study were left feeling exposed in many ways because of his research approach and as a result did not want to be involved in his focus group session. There was little in the way of a trustworthy environment here for Phuong and her students. If Nhung's research project sought to critique and investigate the English language skills of the participants involved, then he had a moral commitment and a duty of care to have ensured that this information was clearly conveyed to his participants during his first encounter with them. If Nhung intended to use film as part of his data collection strategy then it was incumbent on him to have informed Phuong from the beginning that this was his intention. An important criticism of deception then is that participants can feel violated when they have been subject to research procedures that they did not initially agree to (Gillespie, 1991). Feelings of mistrust and anger can be minimised when participants are carefully informed about their role and are clear on what is expected of them during each stage of the research process (Drew, Hardman, & Hosp, 2008).

Deception can also involve the inaccurate portrayal of data findings or sample size (Hammersley & Traianou, 2012). Fabricating, altering or omitting data findings are all examples of deceitful action that can have negative consequences in that it 'corrodes a researcher's integrity and commitment to truth and jeopardises community support for research' (Lawson, 1997, p. 19). Reusing another researcher's data findings and claiming this work as one's own is also viewed as dishonest conduct. In this case, plagiarism occurs where there is no acknowledgement of another person's research through adequate referencing to the author/s work. In addition, researchers who give false information or withhold certain information related to their study are seen to behave in a deceptive way. Asking a participant to engage in an activity that is essentially immoral or dangerous and where a person has been misled on the safety aspect of his/her involvement also counts for 'deception by omission' (Athanassoulis & Wilson 2009). In all of these instances a researcher has a duty of care to ensure that a professional code of conduct is adopted so that the safety of participants is at all times preserved and maintained.

Privacy and Confidentiality

It had been the researcher's last day of observing Phuong's class and taking field notes. The beginning teacher was happy that this project had finally ceased and she looked forward to restoring a sense of connection with her students. The past couple of weeks had been an anxious time in many ways for everyone except Nhung. During the first week Phuong overheard Nhung speaking about her teaching style to another colleague and how much it needed to 'improve'. In a loud voice he went on to explain how his presence in the classroom would help to facilitate remarkable changes in Phuong's ability to engage her students in a more enlightening way. During the second week Phuong returned an English language book to the staff study area. When she walked past Nhung's desk, a desk that other teachers walked by each morning, she came across his field notes. This is what she saw:

Date: 2nd June 2014
Participant Observation Field Notes: Written by Nhung Tran
Teacher Being Observed: Phuong Nguyen: English Language Class
Language Focus: Adjectives and Adverbs
Class: Form Two: 35 Students, 20 girls and 10 boys

Overview of the Class
Today Phuong began her lesson by asking her students to open their textbooks to page 10. She told the class that they would be examining adjectives and adverbs and went on to explain their syntactic function in the English language. Phuong gave a brief introduction on the meanings

associated with these terms and wrote up a few examples on the board. She finished her introduction by writing down a list of exercises that she wanted the students to complete. The class didn't seem interested at all in completing the textbook exercises. I noticed that a couple of boys had big frowns on their faces when they began the grammar exercises and didn't appear to be motivated at all. I also observed that none of the students seemed to want to initiate a conversation around how they could use adjectives and adverbs in everyday English conversations.

Phuong really has a dull presence in the classroom and has no idea of how to embed any higher order thinking skills into her lesson planning. I found the lesson to be quite uninspiring and boring. There is so much more that Phuong could be doing to involve her students in more practical and meaningful ways! Despite me showing her how to embed some CLT strategies into her teaching she has chosen to ignore my suggestions. I find this frustrating and don't understand why she does not want to improve her teaching style!

As demonstrated in the case above, privacy and confidentiality are significant aspects of the conduct of ethical research (Wiles, Crow, Heath, & Charles, 2008). Whilst these terms are often used interchangeably they have their own distinct meanings. Privacy relates to controlling the kind of information that is released about an individual or a group of people who are involved in a research project. Protecting a participant's privacy means controlling the way in which he or she is presented in the public domain (Fouka & Mantzorou, 2011). 'Confidentiality', in contrast, refers to the way in which *data* is managed and stored. This applies to who has access to the data collected and the degree to which data is shared with others outside of the research project. Privacy then is aligned with protecting the individual where confidentiality protects the dissemination of data in ways that minimise participants' exposure to potential scrutiny or harm (Sieber, 1992). With this in mind, researchers have a duty of care to ensure that at all times information that could easily identify a person or community is screened so as to protect their anonymity. Wiles et al., (2008) extends definitions of confidentiality by stating that researchers have a duty of care to ensure that they do not openly discuss or disclose observations or discussions that involve participants in their research studies (p. 418). To do so could raise a number of damaging outcomes that may lead to participants being stigmatised or viewed in a negative way by those outside of the study.

Ethical guidelines and research protocols all emphasise the importance of using pseudonyms during the research process to safeguard the identities of research participants (Smyth & Williamson, 2004). In addition, the term 'data cleaning' is used by Kaiser (2009, p. 5) to describe the process whereby researchers 'remove identifiers to create a clean data set. A clean data set does not contain information that identifies respondents, such as name or address'. However it is worth noting here that removing or changing a name does not automatically mean that a participant's identity or an institution's identity remains anonymous. An individual or institution's identity could be recognised by other people who have access to the published data because of the inclusion of other identifiable information. Researchers therefore need to make a decision as to the kind of information they include and the extent to which this information could lead to deductive disclosure.

Kaiser goes on to assert the need to store such de-identifying identified information in a place that is secure and protected. It is worth noting here that many university research ethics application forms ask that researchers keep their data in a locked cupboard so as to minimise the risk of a participant's anonymity being exposed.[22] In the case of Nhung, leaving his field notes in the public gaze is a serious breach of privacy and confidentially. Nhung did not store his observation notes in a safe place and this seriously compromised his ability to keep Phuong and her students safe from harm. Phuong is likely to seriously doubt her professional capabilities as a result of having read the notes that were taken about her teaching approach. Knowing that there is a strong possibility that other colleagues saw Nhung's negative comments about Phuong is likely to evoke feelings of shame and embarrassment for the graduate teacher. All of these feelings can have a considerable influence on Phuong's ability to foster a collaborative relationship with Nhung and with her peers.

---

2   See the following websites for Canterbury Christ Church University: http://www.canterbury.ac.uk/support/computing-services/Policies-Procedures/Data%20protection%20v2%203.pdf and the University of Aberdeen: http://www.abdn.ac.uk/hsru/documents/Protecting_information_policy_v5_Dec13.pdf

McDermid, Peters, Jackson and Daly (2014, p. 31) discuss the challenges that can arise when research involves subjects where there are pre-existing collegial associations. They contend that 'participants may experience physical and emotional distress and be at risk of reprisal or retaliation if their anonymity is inadvertently breached in their organisations'. There is no doubt that Nhung has considerable status and power at the school; that he can influence the decision that is made by the school principal as to whether or not Phuong is a good teacher to invest in. Phuong's employment situation means that her contract will be unlikely to be renewed if she is labeled or portrayed as an incompetent English language teacher. Job insecurity and unemployment is certainly not what Phuong signed up for when she agreed to participate in Nhung's research. Indeed, Nhung demonstrates all of the signs of a careless and unethical researcher who has no awareness of the destructive impact of his actions on the lives of people surrounding him. His actions serve to remind us that when conducting research in worksites one must acquire a delicate and well thought out approach; that relationships between colleagues can become complex when guidelines and protocols associated with the conduct of ethical research are ignored. Any research that involves colleagues needs to have as its starting point the knowledge that worksites, 'are enmeshed in a network of membership affiliations, and an individual becoming a researcher can set him or her apart and affect relationships with other group members' (McDermid et al., 2014, p. 29). Overall protecting and preserving constructive and respectful relationships is central to the research process. Initiating and maintaining ethical research standards

On the Friday evening following Nhung's departure, Phuong wrote an email to her best friend Trung. In her email she outlined the range of intense emotions that had consumed her throughout her involvement in Nhung's research project. In her email, Phuong outlined why she had found it difficult to embed CLT strategies into her classroom practice and how for the most part, she felt victimised and misunderstood by the researcher. Phuong's email is recorded below:

Dear Tran,

I hope all is well. It has been some time since we have made contact with each other.

I hope you don't mind but I am feeling really angry about a situation that I have been involved in over the past two weeks. I really do need to share this with someone who I trust and I know that you will understand my standpoint and not judge me in a negative way.

Basically I have been involved in a research project and have had a senior teacher observe my classes to assess my proficiency in English language teaching. During this time I have found his presence in my classroom to be quite traumatic. The major reason for this is because I have not been able to adopt some of the teaching strategies (underpinned by a communicative language teaching approach) that he wanted me to use. I know there are reasons for not wanting to teach this way. And I do feel like a failure and a fraud and I really do need to work harder so that I can become a better English language teacher and make my English classes more exciting for my students.

But Tran, the fact remains that my English is not as proficient as it should be. I have only been teaching English for 6 months and I am still not confident in my ability to embed conversational activities into my lessons or to use techniques that may cause too much chatter in the classroom. What I am most concerned about here is that if I allow my students to freely participate in English conversation that I will not be able to understand some of the English terms that might be used. This will embarrass me even further and I have my reputation to uphold if I am to secure a full time position here. This is why I like using grammar books because I feel most comfortable and competent when sharing my knowledge of syntax and language rules. Despite my confidence here, when I tried to tell the researcher about why I like using text-books in my English classes he was quite dismissive of my reasoning. What soon became apparent to me is that he was not prepared to listen to what I had to say. Rather, all he was interested in doing was telling me what I should be doing to motivate my students to want to learn English.

> I feel so confused. I can't go and speak to the Principal about this experience for I fear that he will not renew my contract if he thinks that I am talking negatively about a senior member of staff. I know that by going to the Principal that it will be perceived as undermining Nhung's expertise and research capability. The researcher has a lot of colleagues at this school who respect his work so I also run the risk of being labeled as a troublemaker and of being alienated. I believe that my career is too important so I will keep quiet and will simply have to deal with the undesirable mental state that I am currently in.

is therefore essential to reducing the risk of adverse situations, like those experienced by Phuong, from arising.

Cross-Cultural Representation

Ethical issues often arise when research is conducted in diverse cultural contexts (Mabelle, 2011). The researcher who brings along an ethnocentric stance to the research arena interprets social phenomena in a jaded way. Marshall and Batten (2003, p. 140) support this assertion when they argue that 'the academic perspective, despite some theoretical grounding in diversity, remains an extension of the dominant culture's base of largely European Western Values, ethics and norms'. Researchers who fail to consider the lived experience of participants, choosing instead to be an 'expert' and to have an over-arching sense of power in the field, invariably silence those voices that really matter. Researchers who overlook cultural variance in the way people think and who dismiss alternative viewpoints run the risk of damaging the integrity and reliability of the data findings (Crigger, Holcomb & Weiss, 2001; Liamputtong, 2010). In the case of Nhung, his persistence in espousing a Western philosophy of teaching and learning led him to ignore personal and professional motivations that encourage English language teachers to teach in particular ways. Rather than attempt to understand the cultural narrative that led Phuong to teach the way she did, Nhung chose to exert a sense of power over his interpretation of Phuong's pedagogical approach. The students' reactions to Nhung are also important here in that they too felt cheated and undermined by his approach. This inhibited their eagerness to further elaborate on their perceptions of effective language teaching in a focus group session. This is unfortunate because Nhung never really understands the motivation behind Phuong's resistance to embedding a communicative teaching approach into her practice. As a result his data collection and data analysis is severely hindered. This compromises Nhung's ability to answer the research questions he sets about the role of CLT in EAL classrooms in an authentic and meaningful way.

In his research, Ellis (1994) makes a number of claims as to why many Vietnamese teachers are not willing to incorporate a communicative approach to their teaching. He writes,

> On the surface it seemed that Vietnamese resistance to adopting the communicative approach lay squarely with class sizes, grammar-based examinations, lack of exposure to authentic language etc., however, on closer investigation it became clear that the Vietnamese teachers would have to make radical changes to some of their basic cultural beliefs if they wanted to accommodate the approach being proposed (p. v).

Ellis' draws our attention to the way in which cultural legacies influence the ease at which teachers can shift from one paradigm of teaching to another. Historical legacies, socio-cultural ideologies and institutional systems of power are all significant factors that influence pedagogical approaches in EAL contexts. Harmer (2007, p. 70) further elaborates on the complexities and challenges experienced by EAL teachers when they attempt to integrate CLT methodologies into their teaching. We see this when he argues that the CLT approach favours 'native-speaker teachers' in that there is the expectation that language learning is based on 'a relatively uncontrolled range of language on the part of the student'. The EAL teacher in the communicative classroom is then expected to be able to effectively respond to conversational encounters in ways that demonstrate his or her own proficiency and mastery of the language. If EAL teachers are not so confident in their English pronunciation or language comprehension, they are less likely to want to promote this kind of teaching approach in their classroom. Nhung's failure to delve into the cultural challenges faced by a non-native English speaker in an English language teaching role had implications. First, he was not sensitive to or aware of the rationale behind Phoung's preference for the using textbooks in her class. Second, his lack of cultural awareness meant that he enforced a privileging of one kind of teaching strategy above another. Ethical research does not claim power over a participant's thoughts or actions. Instead ethical research attempts to unpack and examine the phenomena being explored so as to answer the question, 'What is really going on here?'

Research that involves cross-cultural teaching and learning approaches must consider contributing factors that make up the classroom milieu (Marshall & Batten, 2003). Hiep's (2007) study of three Vietnamese teachers and their attempts to implement CLT approaches also highlights the important role that institutions play in facilitating successful teaching and learning outcomes. His research findings indicate that when embedding new pedagogical approaches, Vietnamese EAL teachers need to be supported by 'peers, students and policy makers' and 'should not be left alone in the process'. Ethical research therefore considers systemic and institutional factors that are influencing the success with which goals and outcomes can be achieved. In the case of Nhung, there was a need for his research to be critical of the kinds of resources, leadership, peer-mentoring and time allowance afforded to Phuong during her trialling of the CLT methodology. An absence of this level of critique meant that a superficial level of data collection and data analysis was generated. This resulted in not presenting an accurate view of why Phuong found it difficult to successfully embed CLT teaching activities into her classroom practice.

Cross-cultural research must also inquire into the multiple dimensions that make up participant identities. McNae and Strachan (2010, p. 43) stress the need to challenge and be critical of cross-cultural research that focuses only on ethnic diversity. They assert that culture can also be thought of as 'youth, aged, gay, lesbian, religious, rural, urban, prison, poor, wealthy and differently abled'. Engaging in respectful and responsive dialogue helps researchers to have an understanding of broader contexts that lead people to think and perform in certain ways. Researchers need to also be cognisant of how their political ideologies can impact on the ways in which they interpret and represent social phenomena. For example, researchers who identify with political and social ideologies found in feminism, queer theory, Marxism, post-structuralism, post-colonialism or post-modern theory, will interpret social occurrences through a particular lens. Ensuring that a researcher's ideological standpoint and positionality do not get in the way of an accurate interpretation and portrayal of the data is essential to the conduct of ethical research. Further, when thinking about how researchers interact with participants from different cultural contexts, it is important that political ideologies do not interfere with respectful cultural interactions. For the feminist researcher whose research topic involves dealing with Saudi Arabian officials who have a particular view of the world and women, the researcher needs to be measured, considered and not impose his or her views on the story that is told. It is during the data reporting back phase when the researcher can voice his or her criticality in ways that also take into consideration the cultural situation in which the research has arisen. In summary all kinds of identities need to be considered, represented and understood in ways that an enable a truthful account of the research that has been conducted.

Conclusion

This chapter has discussed the various deliberations that must be considered by a researcher if research is to be conducted in an ethical way. The importance of ensuring that individuals feel safe and are not coerced or deceived into participating in a research project is central to the ethical dimensions of the research process. Ethics, as discussed, involves a critical dimension; to ignore the institutional, cultural, historical and political standpoints that people bring to the research arena, devalues and silences those elements that influence why people respond and behave in particular ways. Essentially, ethical research opens up collaborative and respectful dialogue between the researcher and his or her participants. Making public the lived experiences of participants in ways that bring about transformative change is what effective research is all about—otherwise why do it? If research serves only to reinforce dominant positions that seek to further marginalise and silence individuals who are the least advantaged, then one must question the integrity of the researcher and the motivations for why the research is being conducted in the first place.

Dr. Marcelle Cacciattolo
College of Education
Victoria University

References

Athanassoulis, N., & Wilson, J. (2009). When is deception in research ethical? *Clinical Ethics, 4*(issue number?), 44-49.

Bortolotti, L., & Mameli, M. (2006). Deception in psychology: Moral costs and benefits of unsought self-knowledge. *Account Research, 13*(3), 259-275.

Bouma, G., & Ling, R. (2004). *The research process.* South Melbourne: Oxford University Press.

Crigger, N. J., Holcomb, L., & Weiss, J. (2001). Fundamentalism, multiculturalism, and problems conducting research with populations in developing nations. *Nursing Ethics, 8*(5), 459-469.

Drew, C.J., Hardman, M., & Hosp, J. (2008). *Designing and conducting research in education.* Los Angeles, CA: Sage.

Ellis, G. D. 1994. *The appropriateness of the communicative approach in Vietnam: An interview study in intercultural communication* (Unpublished master's thesis). Faculty of Education, La Trobe University, Melbourne.

Escobedo, C., Guerrero, J., Lujan, G., Ramirez, A., & Serrano, D. (2007). Ethical issues with informed consent. *Bio-Ethics Issues.* Retrieved from: http://cstep.cs.utep.edu/Ezine-Fall2007issue.pdf

Fouka, G., & Mantzorou, M. (2011). What are the major ethical issues in conducting research? Is there a conflict between the research ethics and the nature of nursing? *Health Science Journal, 5*(1), 3-14.

Gillespie R. (1991). *Manufacturing knowledge: A history of the Hawthorne experiments.* Cambridge: Cambridge University Press.

Hammersley, M., & Traianou, A. (2012). *Ethics and qualitative research.* London: Sage.

Harmer, J. (2007). *The practice of English language teaching* (4th ed.). London: Longman.

Hawkins, J., & Emanuel, E. J. (Eds.). (2008). *Exploitation and developing countries: The ethics of clinical research.* Princeton: Princeton University Press.

Hesse-Biber, S., & Leavy, P. (2011). *The practice of qualitative research.* Thousand Oak, CA: Sage.

Hiep, Pham Hoa. (2007). Communicative language teaching: Unity within diversity. *ELT Journal, 61*(3), 193-201.

Hood, S., Kelley, P., & Mayall, B. (1996). `Children as research subjects: A risky enterprise. *Children and Society, 10*(2), 117-128.

Kaiser, K. (2009). Protecting respondent confidentiality in qualitative research. *Qualitative Health Research, 19*(11), 1632-1641.

Kimmel, A. J., Smith, N., & Klein, J. (2010. Ethical decision making and research deception in the behavioral sciences: An application of social contract theory. *Ethics & Behavior, 21*(3), 222-251. doi:10.1080/10508422.2011.5701

Koulouriotis, J. (2011). Ethical considerations in considerations in conducting research with non-native speakers. *TESL Canada Journal 28*(5), 1-15.

Lawson, E. (1997). Deception in research: After thirty years of controversy. In M. Bibby (Ed.), *Review of Australian research in education No. 4: Ethics and education research.* Coldstream, Victoria: Australian Association for Research in Education.

Liamputtong, P. (2010). *Performing qualitative cross-cultural research.* Cambridge: Cambridge University Press.

Locke, T., Acorn, N., & O'Neill, J. (2013). Ethical issues in collaborative action research. *Educational Action Research, 21*(1), 107-123.

Mabelle, V.P. (2011). Ethical dimensions of shared ethnicity, language and immigration experience. *TESL Canada Journal, 5*, 72-79.

Marshall, A., & Batten, S. (2003). *Ethical issues in cross-cultural research.* Retrieved from http://www.educ.uvic.ca/Research/conferences/connections2003/10Marshall105.pdf

McDermid, F., Peters, K., Jackson, D., & Daly, J. (2014) Conducting qualitative research in the context of pre-existing peer and collegial relationships. *Nurse Researcher, 21*(5), 28-33.

McKay, P. (2006). *Assessing young language learners.* Cambridge: Cambridge University Press.

McNae, R.. & Strachan, J. (2010). Researching in cross cultural contexts: A socially just process. *Waikato Journal of Education, 15*(2), 41-54.

Mitchell, I. (2004). Identifying ethical issues in self-study proposals. In J. Loughran (Ed.), *International handbook of self-study of teaching and teacher education practices* (pp. 1393-1442). Dordrecht: Kluwer Academic.

Morrow, V., & Richards, M. (1996). The ethics of social research with children: An overview. *Children and Society, 10*(2), 90-105.

Nicks, S. D., Korn, J. H., & Mainieri, T. (1997). The rise and fall of deception in social psychology and personality research, 1921 to 1994. *Ethics Behaviour, 7*(1), 69-77.

Nyame-Asiamah, F., & Patel, N. (2009). *Research methods and methodologies for studying organizational learning.* Paper presented at European and Mediterranean Conference on Information Systems, Izmir.

Orb, A., Eisenhauer, L., & Wynaden, D. (2001), Ethics in qualitative research. *Journal of Nursing Scholarship, 33*(1), 93-96.

Pierce, R. (2009). What a tangled web we weave: Ethical and legal implications of deception in recruitment. *Journal of Clinical Research Best Practices, 5*(8), 1-14.

Sieber, J. E. (1992). *Planning ethically responsible research: A guide for students and inernal review boards* (vol. 31). Newbury Park: Sage Publications.

Smith, A. B., & Taylor, N. J. (2000). The sociocultural context of childhood: Balancing dependency and agency. In A. B. Smith, N. J. Taylor & M. M. Gollop (Eds.). *Children's voices. Research, policy and practice* (pp.1-17). Auckland, NZ: Pearson Education Ltd.

Smyth, M., & Williamson, W. (Eds.) (2004). *Researchers and their 'subjects': Ethics, power, knowledge and consent.* Bristol: Policy Press.

Stocker, J. (2012). Ethical challenges in teacher research: The case of an ESP foreign language course in Taiwan. *Taiwan International ESP Journal, 3*(2), 51-72.

Tierney, W.G. (1997). Border Guards: Ethnographic Fiction and Social Science'. In M. Fine, L. Weis, L. P. Pruitt & A. Burns (Eds.), *Off white: Reading on society, race and culture* (pp. 110-20). New York, NY: Routledge.

Wiles, R., Crow, G., Heath, S., & Charles, V. (2008). The management of confidentiality and anonymity in social research, *International Journal of Social Research Methodology, 11*(5), 417-428.

Chapter Five

Disenfranchisement and Empowerment in an EAL Educational Setting

MARK VICARS

This chapter explores the usefulness of a critical action research approach for developing English Language skills in English as an additional language teaching contexts. It situates local culture as a space from which to stage interventions in institutionally disenfranchising English language curricula and pedagogy

Learning about learning, has within this paradigm, I suggest, a duty of care to be mindful of the power and privileges that are brought to and operate in and through the pedagogical encounter. A critical approach to understanding EAL pedagogy is one that increasingly draws upon and recognizes the utility of the plurality of Englishes (Baker, 2012) as opposed to a monolithic singular English. Local expressions and uses of English are rarely represented in traditional language learning classrooms and the concept of Englishes in language classrooms is seldom encouraged. In this chapter I tell a story of what happened when they were placed at the centre of the language learning experience as a productive space for interruption.

Affirming the presence of local culture in language teaching methodologies and language teaching materials positions learner agency and cultural capital as an organizing principal as a driver in the pedagogic encounter.

M. Vicars et al. (eds.), *The Praxis of English Language Teaching and Learning (PELT)*, 75–89.

In this chapter I draw on data taken from a study with Thai secondary students who were studying in an international school in Bangkok. The thematic concerns are of re/motivating and engaging young non- native speakers with English language learning by drawing on local cultural resources to facilitate peer to peer learning.

Criticality in Action Research

The language-learning classroom, it could be argued, has a culture that habituates and inscribes binary models of language teaching and learning. Morgan and Ramanathan, (2005, p.154) have remarked how:

> As "subjects-in-discourse", both students and teachers are differentially positioned—in multiple and often contradictory ways .... complexity arises in the textual forging of schooled voices, the merging—to various degrees of success—of cultural memories and prior forms of language socialization with conscious and unconscious strategies of imitation, accommodation, or opposition to the dominant norms of the academic discourse community

Anyone that has endeavored to learn an additional language will remember encounters of the feel of how the Other is made present within the pedagogic space of the language learning classroom. Positioned in relation to didactic rhetoric, pedagogies of control and structural drills are all too a familiar experience for learners in the unreconstructed EAL classrooms. A regulatory routine of drip-feed pedagogy often characterizes the practice of what at best can be described as moribund language ideology in practice. As language educators too, we are often compelled to put in place a language ideology pedagogy as it has mandated approval by institutional hierarchies. However, as Morgan and Ramanathan (2005, p.154) have noted:

> As "subjects-in-discourse" we are each (students, teachers, researchers, scholars in ELT) in positions where we can turn the critical lens on ourselves to where we hold everything about our professional lives to the light: our teaching, choice of pedagogic materials, discipline's orientations, valued genres, socialization practices.

And Luke, 2004 (p.26) notes how:

> To be critical is to call up for scrutiny, whether through embodied action or discourse practice, the rules of exchange within a social field. To do so requires an analytic move to self-position oneself as Other even in a market or field that might not necessarily construe or structurally position one as Other . . . . This doubling and positioning of the self from dominant text and discourse can be cognate, analytic, expository, and hypothetical, and it can, indeed, be already lived, narrated, embodied, and experienced. (Luke, 2004, p. 26)

Language pedagogy as informed by language ideology in a critical paradigm becomes a significant problematic as it situates the language learner as an empty vessel to be filled-up by the language educator who as the banker of the target language knowledge can then assess 'progress' and 'proficiency' with a norm referenced standardizing criteria. Language practices, on the other hand rarely comply with pedagogical orthodoxies as they draw on and privilege how language is used in 'real-'life'. Language practices are messy, they do not neatly conform as they make use of and rely on the local contexts in which language is situated (Spolsky, 2002).

This chapter in contesting orthodoxies about the learning of English as an additional language is framed by a pedagogy of interruption of the normal; of a singular logic that advocates a pluralized notion of literacies (Morgan and Ramanathan, 2005, p.152). Inserting the presence of local culture and being pedagogically prepared to 'go with' the 'unplanned', can I suggest in EAL settings draw in and upon 'identity, social participation and positioning and engagement [as] important cultural and subcultural practices [as these are] central to the lives of individuals and to the society in which they participate (Merchant and Carrington, 2009, p 64).

The project that is described was conducted with a class of nineteen children that had the previous semester transitioned from primary to secondary school in an international school in Bangkok, Thailand. It had the aim of motivating students who had become disenfranchised in their learning by a language policy that had an ideological aim of promoting a standardized English that was connected to raising attainment in external examinations. It was an ill-conceived pedagogical response to the difficulties the teachers were having in promoting the use of English by Students. Policing English as the language of instruction and the mandating of 'English Only' throughout the school was the punitively enforced through the disciplining measures of:

- detentions for being caught speaking a mother tongue language
- English language only zones of the school
- name and shame—students caught speaking mother tongue had their names published in a weekly newsletter that was sent home to parents

The impact of these measures became visibly apparent in the increased detentions and an ever increasing roll of the 'named and shamed' which had a detrimental result. The more linguistically capable students became more anxious and the less English proficient students became increasingly reticent to use the little English language they knew. As the semester weeks passed, English language fatigue materialized amongst many of the students as teacher-talk came to dominate classrooms. As an early doubter of the institutions language policy, my compulsion to intervene in and disrupt the policy was driven out of i) a sense of injustice ii) an ethic of care towards the students and iii) my frustration with increasing levels of disengagement in the classroom. As the students different ways with words (Heath, 1983) did not have a place any more in the classroom the silences became deafening. I willingly and willfully ignored the continued practice of the use of Thai/lish and English in my classroom and it was whilst patrolling the yard in their recreation time and observing the students linguistic heteroglossia that I came upon the idea to move this language play in to the classroom to create possibilities rather than reinforce dead-end certainties.

Learning About Being Learner-Centered

The more I had observed the students use of English language in their recreational spaces, the more I became more convinced of the need to ' ...respect the knowledge that children bring to language and learning' (Campbell and Green, 2003, p.6). I started to think through the possibilities of drawing on their situated informal language practices to reconstruct the formal binaries that positioned and located them as at best unaccomplished and at worst in need of remedial help. Nunan (1988.p.179) has described the turn to learner–centredness in the learning of language as 'requiring learners to participate and negotiate actively in meaningful interaction in order to interpret and construct meaning by themselves and I started to consider what options were available. Previously in my classroom, I had incorporated dramatic play as learner-centred acitivity and Vitz (1984) has noted how children with limited language confidence and proficiency, who participated in drama activities, had an increase in a willingness to use the target language in social interactions. McGregor, Tate and Robinson (1977) have noted how educational drama can create continuous moments of arrival and bring forth new configurations of language use and the productivity for dramatic play for modelling literacy behaviors. Scarcella (1987) suggests it is in the aspect of authenticity in the dramatic action that promotes language acquisition and the motivation for maintenance. Thinking through the fluidity involved in the learning of an additional language, the need for repeated opportunities to test-out the target language and to refer back to the mother tongue solidified my thinking that drama in the classroom would be a productive tool for developing a language practice approach.

Initially I set out to identify the issues that the language policy of the school had generated and these were visibly apparent in :

- low student self-esteem in their oral English language ability

- passive role in classrooms

- low confidence in their written English

- high levels of anxiety when asked to read or write in English

- a concern with the mechanics of construction/ grammar

Freire (1988, pp.72-73) remarked how:

> Educators need to know what happens in the world of children with whom they work. They need to know the universe of their dreams, the language with which they skillfully defend themselves from the aggressiveness of their world and what they know independently of the school and how they know it.

I began to put in action a plan for change.

Acting-up

Starting the project, I explained to the students how over the next 7 weeks of the semester we would be creating a drama based on a theme of their choice. There followed a brief discussion about a Thai film that had received extensive media coverage: Bangrachan an epic drama that recounted the historical conflict and invasion of the ancient capital of Ayuthaya by the Burmese. The majority of the students had seen the film as the narrative had been popularized and contemporized with special effects and elaborately constructed battle scenes. As the students started to collaboratively mind map, in visual form the key events that were to form the basis of the drama, they intuitively took up active positions in the negotiation and planning demonstrating how collaborative work can facilitate:

- involvement at conceptual levels
- participate in conversations about events and things
- hear models of English language
- experiment as they learn with the language structures to express meaning (Cinamon, 1994, p.73)

An overview of this process is outlined in table 5.1.

As a class, we collaboratively decided on the focus of the drama and I then introduced the students to drama techniques of -tableaux: a freeze frame that captures or presents an image of an event or situation;-working in role: being asked to act 'as if' they are a particular character and to think, make decisions, draw conclusions, make connections and improvise in role;-hot seating; acting out characters from a story and answering questions about that character in role with detail ;-improvisation: un rehearsed, spontaneous action and asked them to consider how they could be used in the drama to show and tell plot and character development.

At the start of each lesson the students in groups prepared tableaux's that provided an overview of the plot events that were to be improvised that session. The tableaux's generated much discussion about the drama but also about the type of language and the genre that would be needed. Getting the students to think through the drama about the language features and text

Focus ➡	Process ➡	Language Work
Getting started	Tableux and working out of role. Reflection.	Stimulate reflections; promote deeper understanding and response to narrative events. Explicit focus on character, plot and setting. Peer to peer scaffolding of written responses
Setting context	Collaborate working in role (Teacher and Students. Hot Seating	Creating learning context: group work, oral work and personal response
Building roles	In role response to dramatic events	Moving beyond surface meaning; vocabulary development, life to text, text to life focus
Building commitment	Out of role reflections; challenging and eliciting contributions- in role writing	Generating audiences for written work, developing context and purpose for writing
Building background story	Integrating written artifacts in to the drama	Consolidation of understanding of narrative construction of :plot and character.
Owning the material	In role responses to text	Consolidation of understanding of narrative construction of :plot and character.
Building Belief	Tableux, teacher out of role support; reflection and hot seating	Examination of drama from different points of view
Challenging assumptions and redefining contexts	Improvisations	Negotiating text, drafting and editing process
Reflections on the process	Teacher and students working in role	
Responding to views of others	In role: What do we know? Out of role: How can we use this knowledge?	
Developing a new focus	Synthesis of knowledge and skills in language practice	

Table 5.1 An overview to using process drama in an EAL setting

types was a significant break through and became an on-going pedagogic objective.

Prior to the drama commencing, the type and range of classroom talk was limited by and confined within and teacher/student interaction. The concept of 'losing face' by getting the language wrong prevented the students from freely entering in to classroom based discussions. I had become frustrated at the lack of involvement in speaking and listening activities and as the students became accustomed to the routine of creating and commenting on the tableaux, I stepped back and in my 'out-of role' observation noted how focused tableaux work that primarily was visual was providing a platform for meaningful and spontaneous dialogue and for authentic information-gap interactions. The tableaux's facilitated life-to-text/ text-to life talk and were motivating the students to initiate and sustain communication in English, Linnenberg (1997, p.66) has noted how:

> Tableux are useful for introducing the idea of images and focusing students' attention on a particular aspect of the topic. It paves the way to deciphering those images. Tableaux can reveal the specific in the general. This practice also encourages selectivity and economy of expression while developing symbolic thought by stopping the action. Tableaux give time for the student to reflect on the topic and encourages discussion about the meanings behind the action.

As the drama developed so did the language focus and expression. There were occasions when the students experienced 'stuckedness' but these became opportunities for authentic engagement with thinking through and in English language. As the drama narrative unfolded, the language demands escalated and dictionaries and thesauruses were reached for in search of synonyms and antonyms as bridges to find better expression. The students were working with words in ways that previously had been absent in the classroom and as they produced language of : description, instruction, explanation, justification, persuasion, exploration, expression the physical experiencing of language in process was helping the students to reconstruct their experience of English language use.

The drama progressed throughout the semester and as the students worked more in-role they started to produce a range of written texts that were incorporated back in to the dramatic play. They started writing letters, speeches, diaries, interrogation questions and reports. Each of these text types were generated by the students in -role in the drama. In the research journal I was keeping, I noted how the drama was making meaningful pathways in to English, as it was embedded in their decision making activities and was associated with the status of their characters and their involvements in plot developments. The focus around text type became a regular feature for discussion in each of the sessions. Issues of grammar and syntax became more important as the students developed their repertoire of literacy behaviors as readers and writers and I recorded in my journal the increase in confidence, enthusiasm and motivation to get involved in speaking/listening and reading/ writing tasks such as make vocabulary lists, search in dictionaries, draft and edit on the computers to publish and print their storied reconstruction of Bangrachan.

The Dramatic Enactment of the Conflict of the Village of Bangrachan

An elderly monk collecting alms enters the village of Bangrachan and tells the headman that on his travels he has seen Burmese soldiers gathering in the hills and mountains surrounding their village. The headman sends out messengers to gather the villages working in the rice fields, fishing the rivers and in general going about their daily business. Once the village is assembled, it is decided that the most able-bodied of the men should be sent on a spying and information gathering mission to find out how many of the Burmese soldiers there are in hiding. In the meantime, the villagers' organize themselves to erect a defence and tasks are allotted. Bamboo is collected to build a protective fence around the village and in the midst of this task the spies return and tell of the increasing number of Burmese soldiers amassing in the mountains. They tell the villagers of overhearing plans to attack the village, kill the men and take the women and children prisoner. The monk leads the village in prayer to Buddha during which an itinerant musician enters the village and asks why the villagers are not working in the rice fields. The villagers explain their situation and ask the musician if he has seen any unusual activity on his travels. He says he has heard rumors and suggests the idea of sending for help. The villagers ask the monk for help in writing a letter to the King of Siam in the capital and a meeting is called amongst the villagers to discuss the content of the letter. The monk suggests he deliver the letter to the King himself as he will be protected by his religious status. In the meantime, he suggest that the villagers prepare themselves and the village against attack. As the villagers make themselves busy building fences

and making weapons, the headman is discovered stealing food in prepera-
tion for his escape. The villagers are called together to discuss what should
be done and the headman is put on trial. They appoint a prosecution and
defence and an outcome is reached. The headman is demoted and put in
stocks and the village convenes to discuss the merits of the candidates for the
appointment of a new headman. Once elected the new headman calls for an
inventory of the village supplies and preparations continue for the defence
against the Burmese invasion. One of the women who has been working in
the field rushes to announce that her heavily pregnant friend has gone in to
labor and a birthing group must be formed to deliver the baby and a naming
ceremony must be arranged. The baby is named 'Inin' which means sun and
his birth is taken as an omen of good fortune. During the naming ceremony,
the monk returns and informs the villagers the King cannot spare troops to
defend the village and they will have to rely on their own resources. Shortly
after the village is attacked by the Burmese, the men are captured, the stock
piled food stolen and the village is ransacked.

Three months later the villagers are weak from hunger, the monk has
been killed and the baby has died and multiple burial ceremonies have been
performed. The decision is made to attacked the Burmese soldiers under
cover of darkness and a plan is developed to burn the Burmese out of the
hills. The attack is successful, the soldiers are defeated and the villagers cel-
ebrate their victory in song and with poems that tell the story of the village
of Bangrachan.

Reflecting Practices

Unsettling the everyday narratives of classroom practice especially of 'Frontal
teaching that is the kind of teaching that required an authoritarian aura…
and a distance between teacher and student ensures a hierachical set-up'
(Kupfer, 2000, p. 150) can be risky. Zuber-Skerrit, (2001, p. 7) remarked
that any form of reflexive inquiry has the 'aim to know, understand, improve
or change a particular social situation or context for the benefit of the people
who are also the participants (not just subjects) in the inquiry and who are
affected by the results and the solution'. Reflecting on the language learning
throughout the drama, I started to realize how only a few weeks previous to

starting the drama, the majority of the students had articulated how English was:-something only used in school

- that it had to be formal
- that it was difficult
- that there was a ear of getting it wrong
- that it generated feelings of anxiety
- about getting the grammar correct
- difficult
- boring

The dramatic reenactment of Bangrachan had impacted on these beliefs and attitudes and my pedagogic role by being in the drama assisted me in problem solving as a partner and had given me the opportunities to closely scaffold the drafting, revising and reflecting process in English. Initially concerned and unsure about the pedagogic benefits of this position, Witkin (1974) stressed the importance of the teacher being present in the drama at the start and to have duel roles as teacher/co-learner in order to initiate the learning experiences.

Pedagogic culture when thought of as primarily being about the transmission of knowledge situates a restrictive binary that at the learning/ teaching interface frames ways of being, belonging and speaking as an educator: we are supposed to know. Admitting that we may not know or may not be sure of the most productive way to teach can be an unsettling thought. Doyle, (1993, p. 132) notes:

> One of the hardest things for teachers to do is to share the process of learning with students. All our professional training and thinking is in the assumption that we as teachers are supposed to know.

The drama indicated to me how:

> A different model in EAL settings is required-one that is based on partnership with students and teachers in which the responsibility for selecting and organizing the tasks to be engaged in is share. EAL classrooms should be places in which the curriculum is negotiated ... where students have a part in determining the goals to be aimed for and the procedures to be followed. Wells (1987, p.129)

At the end of the drama, I invited the students to discuss their experiences of participation and they commented how, in relation to using English they felt more confident and prepared in the following aspects:

- get ideas with which to start writing;
- use contextual vocabulary;
- using Thai to think through ideas;
- knowing different genres;
- not being anxious to make mistakes

During the process, I journaled daily and the incremental differences in motivation and engagement through the semester and noted the following:

- the students had become better in writing across a range of genres and text types
- the students has started to produce texts that demonstrated increased ability to write imaginatively and produce narratives that were coherent interms f grammar and syntax
- there was an increased use of literary techniques to achieve particular effects
- there was increased evidence of the students using complex sentences to extend, link and develop ideas
- the students showed awareness of the reader in the editing stage
- the students were using persuasive techniques and rhetorical devices in their speaking work
- the students had become better in the planning and drafting stages of writing and were self-evaluating their written texts to further shape and craft their texts

The English language benefits of the drama had become known to me throughout the process but the long lasting effect was in the change in classroom culture. The students were and continued to be much more willing to have a go and engage in tasks that previously had been perceived as to difficult and in which English language had been a barrier to engagement.

Conclusion

English language teaching has for too many years ways been the tojan horse of colonizing cultures as demonstrably evident in the hegemony of scholarship from BANA countries (Britain, Australia and North America) and evidenced in production of Western centric English language learning programs and resources. Krachru's Three Circles Model of World Englishes (1985) has represented the changing distribution and functions of the English language globally.

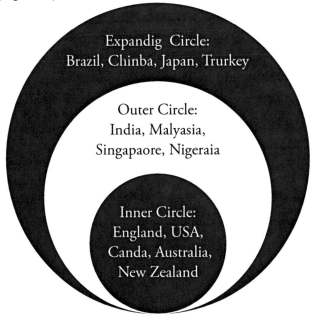

Figure 5.2 Kachru S (1985, 1992) Three Circles Mode

This figure raises the importance of having a critical awareness of the spread of English and of the 'ideological dimensions surrounding the global spread of English (Park and Wee, 2009, p.1-2). English is not only confined to its native speakers and as Baker (2012) has noted Thailand's location in the expanding circle in which it is used for intercultural communication is as a norm dependent country and he indicated how the content of ELT needs to move away from a focus on inner circle Anglo-American varieties of English. A culturally responsive mode of language teaching, one that helps elicit students' stories, opinions, values, and interests as a catalyst for learning, is fundamental to a critical approach. It can textualize the spaces of the classroom with an everyday logic of the participants' English language behaviors by pedagogically acknowledging the lived-through experience/connection with, and to, a text (Rosenblatt, 1938/1968, 1978). Reworking language pedagogy out of a language practice model necessitated moving beyond a normative classroom habitus. This involved resisting the usual disciplining habits of desk, chair, worksheet, and whiteboard. In this project, I replaced the established routines and tools of an EAL class with a playfulness that made time for interruptions and digressions. As the students moved, literally, in and out of their texts of identity as second language learners what they did with and around texts had much to do with being/becoming accomplished in practicing and refining being language learners. This chapter has grappled with some of the questions that every English language teacher will have been exposed to through, and by, their students'. As I endeavored to negotiate my positions/identities as a teacher, I came to recognize that my liminality in the process was increasingly informed by, and contoured through participation as a co- discussant. Refrained from being constrained by a singular logic of practice that would have me choose an either/or position from which to participate, observe and make meaning. My teaching was focused on pedagogically developing and sustaining threads of connection between the students, their social worlds, and these crafty and crafted pedagogical relationships transgressed the authority of, teacher/learner, teacher/researcher, and English/Englishes.

Dr. Mark Vicars
College of Education
Victoria University

References

Baker, W. (2012). English as a lingua franca in Thailand: Characterisations and implications, *Englishes in Practice* (1).

Campbell, R., & Green, D. (Eds). (2003). *Literacies and learners: current perspectives* (3nd ed). French Forest: Australia: Prentice Hall.

Cinamon, D. (1994). Bilingualism and oracy. In S. Brindley (Ed) *Teaching English*: London: Routledge.

Doyle, C. (1993). *Raising curtains on education: Drama as a site for crticial pedagogy.* Westport Connecticut: Bergin & Garvey.

Freire, P. (1988). *Teachers as cultural workers.* Oxford: West View Press.

Heath, S. (1993). Inner city life through drama: Imagining the language classroom. *TESOL Quarterly, 27*(2) 177-192

Kachru, B. B. (1985). Standards, codification and sociolinguistic realism: The English language in the outer circle. In R. Quirk & H. G. Widdowson (Eds.), *English in the world: Teaching and learning the language and literature* (pp. 11-30). Cambridge: Cambridge University Press.

Kupfer, R. (2000). Retracing my journey towards self-acceptence and effectiveness as a lesbian teacher. In J. Ritchie & D. Wilson (Eds) *Teacher narratives as critical inquiry: Rewriting the script.* New York: Teachers College Press.

Linnenberg, V. (1997). *Dramatizing writing: Reincorporating delivery in the classroom.* New Jersey: Lawrence Erlbaum.

Luke, A. (2004). Two takes on the critical. In B. Norton & K. Toohey (Eds.), *Critical pedagogies and language learning* (pp. 21-29). Cambridge: Cambridge University Press.

McGregor, L., Tate, M., & Robinson, K. (1977). *Report of the schools council drama teaching project.* London: Heinemann.

Merchant, G. & Carrington, V. (2009). Editorial, *Literacy, 43*(2) 63-64.

Morgan, B., & Ramanathan, V. (2005). Critical loyeracies and language education: Global and local perspectives. *Annual Review of Applied Linguistics*, 25, 151-169.

Park, J. S-Y, & Wee, L. (2009). The three circles redux: A market-theoretic perspective on World Englishes. *Applied Linguistics, 30*(3), 389-406.

Nunan, D. (1988). *The learner-centred curriculum: a study in second language teaching.* Cambridge/ New York/Melbourne: Cambridge University Press.

Rosenblatt, L. (1968). *Literature as exploration.* (Revised ed.) New York, NY: Noble & Noble. (Original work published 1938)

Sacrcella, R. (1987). Socio-drama for social interaction. In M.Lang & J. Richards (Eds) *Methodology in TESOL.* New York: Newbury House.

Spolsky, B. (2002). Globalisation, language policy and a philosophy of English language education for the 21ˢᵗ Century. *English Teaching 57*(4) 3-26.

Vitz, K. (1984). The effects of creative drama in English as a second language. *Childens theater review,* 33 (2) 23-26.

Wells, G. (1987). *The meaning makers: children learning language and using language to learn.* London: Hodder & Stoughton.

Witkin, R. (1974). *The intelligence of feeling.* London: Heinemann.

Zuber-Skerrit. O. (2001). Action learning and action research: paradigms, praxis and programs. In S. Sankara, B. Dick & R. Passfield (Eds) *Effective change management through action research and action learning: concepts, perspectives processes and applications.* Southern Cross University Press. Lismore, Australia.

Chapter Six

Fundamentals of Quantitative Research in the Field of Teaching English as a Foreign Language

ANTHONY WATT

Introduction: Why Do Quantitative Research in English as a Foreign Language?

Adopting a quantitative approaches in researching teaching English as a Foreign Language (EFL) will achieve much the same purpose as utilising this methodology in the broader fields of education and psychology. Thinking beyond the stereotype of quantitative designs being only applicable to experiments or data collections of a scientific nature is critical in creating opportunities for new knowledge and information in the domain. The renowned psychological and educational researcher Lee Cronbach provided a valuable perspective as to how quantitative educational research framed in the true scientific method may not always be feasible.

> The habits of the psychologist and biologist do not fit research on classroom instruction. Rats receiving a drug or placebo are properly considered to be independent subjects; what one rat does has no effect on the score of the next (unless the experimenter somehow introduces correlated errors). Students in a class, however, do not provide independent evidence. What the class experiences goes beyond the treatment specified by the experimenter (Cronbach, 1976, p. 10).

M. Vicars et al. (eds.), *The Praxis of English Language Teaching and Learning (PELT)*, 91–114.

Although research in the education domain has recently deviated from a focus on the quantitative approach, with a greater emphasis on qualitative methods, the use of numbers can be a very useful tool, either as part of a larger project that employs multiple methods or as a basis for a complete piece of work (Berry, 2005). Brown (2011) suggested that research in the area of EFL involves a systematic and principled inquiry of an area of interest. Furthermore, he defined quantitative research as involving studies that focus on "counting things and the patterns that emerge from those counts" (p. 192).

If we consider EFL within the tenet of critical pedagogy, an amalgam description could be considered as the development of communicative abilities in English and the ability to apply them to developing a critical awareness of the world and the capacity to act for positive change and equitable outcomes for all (Crookes & Lehner, 1998). Quantitative research practices can play an important role in generating evidence to substantiate the viability of this goal, or evaluate exemplars of how EFL teaching and learning practices are aligned with the critical pedagogy philosophy.

Quantitative Research Desing in EFL

Trochim (2006) defined research design as "the glue that holds the research project together. A design is used to structure the research, to show how all of the major parts of the research project—the samples or groups, measures, treatments or programs, and methods of assignment" (p. NA). In support of this endeavour a range of descriptors exist that can be utilised to categorise quantitative research designs suitable for the EFL domain. It is useful to consider these designs along a continuum from the simple through to the more complex. It then becomes the responsibilities of the researcher or team when developing the project to determine the level of complexity required to achieve the research goals. De Vaus (2001) outlined two straightforward questions that can serve as the stimulus to establishing the design framework: (a) What is going on (descriptive research)?; and (b) Why is it going on (explanatory research)?. Furthermore, design can also be considered against the following classifications: (a) Descriptive which involves describing the information being collected using measures such as surveys or assessments records; (b) Associational, which further than description by attempting to determine how the characteristics assessed are related so can better understand phenomena; and (c) Intervention, a more complex approach whereby through intervening and evaluating resultant effects, change in the characteristics of interest can be established (Fraenkel & Wallen, 2011).

High quality literature related to research designs in the social sciences, education and EFL currently exists (e.g., Brown, 2011; Fraenkel, Wallen, & Hyun, 2011; Trochim, 2006). In considering relevant work, the following set of designs that can be applied in the context of EFL will be described individually in greater detail. These designs are descriptive, correlational, comparative, causal, quasi-experimental, and experimental.

Descriptive Designs

Descriptive designs are a necessary element of all quantitative research and can serve as an independent study, or more commonly as the platform on which to construct subsequent analyses. Descriptive research confirms or rejects patterns in the information collected, promotes theoretical discussion of observed data, directs the subsequent design of cause and effect studies, and provides an important base framework for interpreting and generalizing results derived from more complex designs (e.g., inferential, experimental) (McEwan, 2008). The data generated within these designs details scores, behaviours, human characteristics, occurrences, equipment counts, outcomes etc. and is derived from descriptive statistics such as frequency, percentages, mean, mode, median, range, and standard deviation (Brown, 2005). A simple descriptive design could involve determining the country of origin frequencies of the individuals who are completing an off shore course in ESL. Results could generate information that could serve to allow course instructor to set up tutorial groups of individuals of a similar background or indeed work to diversify the groups by assigning members of different nationalities to different groups. Although the simplest research design, descriptive findings can often be the most readily accessible to students and researchers with less of a background in quantitative methods.

Correlational Designs

The correlational design is used to examine the relationship or degree of association between two or more characteristics, attributes, numbers, or quantities that can be measured or counted. Correlational designs can only provide information in regards to the existence of an association and do not allow the researchers to infer a cause. Researchers who incorporate a correlational research design do not manipulate any elements of interest but collect data on existing factors or characteristics and typically examine any relationships within a single defined group (Johnson, 2000). This design allows for any two scores collected to be compared, however, it is important to use logic to support evaluating the association. The basic reporting statistic is a correlation value, in which the higher the value the stronger the link (e.g., height and weight), whereas in the negative direction, the value indicates the scores operate in opposite directions (e.g., days of sunshine and precipitation). Correlational designs also allow for the prediction of how a score might influence another score in the future. Many studies in education and EFL could be developed around the correlation design. For example, evaluating the relationship between the students entry level English skills and time required to complete an ESL program of studies establish. Furthermore, entry level English skills could also be compared with scores on the first course exam, and provide information that could assist in predicting course performance based on entry level English skills. As with descriptive designs, correlational designs are considered a simple quantitative approach.

Causal-Comparative Designs

Causal-Comparative designs involve research in which the researcher attempts to answer questions in regard to simple differences between two or more groups (Lauer, 2004). The contrast effects have already occurred and the researcher attempts to determine whether one characteristic may have influenced another characteristic. The main difference between this design and the early designs discussed is that the researcher may now put forward opinions or reasonable inferences regarding the cause of any possible findings (Gay et al., 2006). Investigators will typically decide to use a causal-comparative design when the groups (and associated variable) involved cannot be manipulated for ethical and practical reasons. The forming of groups is based on natural occurrence and where the characteristic of interest is present or absent (Gall, Borg, & Gall, 2003) and the observation relates to natural characteristics and not manipulated variables. For example, it may only be possible to compare scores regarding different tutorial groups on the basis of assessments that constitute part of a set course. Students may not have the time to prepare for a specific measure developed for the research, or the researchers may not have the time or funding to manage administration of a separate measure. In this case the findings may tentatively allow us to infer that differences in scores between tutorial groups may be due to teaching or teacher characteristics. Simple causal-comparative designs provide an excellent source of evidence upon which to base the development of more complex manipulation or intervention studies.

Quasi-Experimental Designs

Quasi-experimental design often used in educational research because investigators cannot always randomly assign participants to groups in particular settings or manipulate an intervention because of ethics and system constraints. It is not typically appropriate to withhold or administer an educational technique to one group and purposely do the opposite to a similar group. Therefore, a quasi-experimental design could be described as a best attempt at an experiment when it is impossible, or not reasonable, to meet all the criteria of a true experiment. Yet, there is still an attempt to isolate the treatment so that inferences can best be attributed to the treatment or intervention. Typically, as its primary goal, research incorporating quasi-experimental methodologies attempts to answer questions such as: "Does a treatment or intervention have an impact?" and "What is the relationship between program practices and outcomes?" (Dimsdale & Kutner, 2004). In quasi-experimental studies, researchers attempt to control for differences between non-randomly assigned groups in a number of ways. Although groups are not randomly assigned the design may necessitate the matching of groups (e.g., year one ESL students with year one ESL students). Additionally, the investigators can incorporate statistical controls such as pretesting of the matched groups before the treatment. It is likely in research within the ESL domain, that the quasi-experimental design will serve as an appropriate approach in which new ideas or techniques could be evaluated.

Experimental Designs

The critical element in experimental design is the random assignment of the participants to one of several treatment or intervention groups. A basic experimental design involves randomly assigning the members of the group of interest to either an experimental cohort, that receives a treatment, or the control cohort, who receive no treatment. Anderman (2006) succinctly describes the principal goal of an experimental design that reflects an education context.

> differences in treatment between the experimental and the control group are tightly controlled, and if subsequent to the experiment there are measurable differences between the two groups that were not present before the experiment, then researchers often conclude that the experimental manipulation "caused" the differences to occur (p 5)

In ESL research, an experimental design could involve the random assignment of a second year Masters of TESOL class into three groups. All students are using a text books and receive the ascribed lectures and tutorials and have completed their first course progress language test. Treatment group one will access a new language tutorial website for three weeks following the course progress language test, treatment group two will join a language conversation club for three works, and the control group will complete the course in standard delivery. After four weeks the students will complete the second language test of the course. Test score differences between the three groups will be considered as an indication of the efficacy of the treatments. It should be recognized that in experimental research in education settings that many other factors can influence results, such as members of the control group working harder in the second phase, or preparing more effectively for the second test.

Planning a Quantitative Research Project in EFL

Quantitative research is typically framed by the important decisions made prior to the commencement of a project. Critical areas for consideration include the formulation of aims that connect to theory, detailing of specific quantifiable research questions, and the selection and implementation of a logical and viable design.

General Aims of the Research in EFL

Developing aims in quantitative research necessitates substantive reflection and evaluation of both theory and previous research that match the general ideas being proposed. Further to this, in the ESL domain aims can also be derived from the observation and experience of practical problems in the field (Trochim, 2006). Once an idea is formulated, the researcher should establish that literature and previous research exist that will support planning. At many levels of quantitative research it is acceptable to replicate a previous study using different sample demographics or to pursue a alternative interpretation of a theory or construct. Aims, therefore, should constitute the project team's ideas in an area of ESL research that are detailed in a manner that others from the ESL field can easily comprehend. Similar to the aims, in quantitative research a hypothesis can also be proposed. The hypothesis is still a general statement without connection to measurement or findings, but represents a specific statement of the predictive thinking that underpins the aims of the research (Fraenkal et al. 2011).

Quantitative Research Questions in EFL

Research questions will serve as the main link between the theoretical or practical aims of investigation and the capacity to collect and analyse data that reflects the aims (Fraenkel et al., 2011). The research questions need to be fully developed prior to the final selection of a methodology or sample (Anderman, 2006). Fraenkal et al. (2011) proposed that research questions should be: (a) feasible, capable of investigation using available resources; (b) clear and specifically defined in operational terms; and (c) developed from definitions recognizable within the field of research.

Specific details of research questions should integrate descriptions of the sample, the variables, and the analysis. Sample information should pertain to demographics elements (e.g., boys or girls, country of origin etc.) or grouping characteristics (e.g., treatment or control, grade 8 or grade 9). Variables also need to be clearly articulated within the research question. In quantitative design the main types of variables (i.e., elements of the research that can vary) are (a) Independent-the cause (demographic characteristic; manipulated, treatment or experimental variable); (b) Dependent -the effect (measured or outcome variable); (c) Quantitative (variables measured as a matter of degree using real numbers, i.e. age, number kids); (d) Categorical (no variation… either in a category or not, i.e. gender, hair color); (e) Extraneous or uncontrolled independent variables (Fraenkal et al. 2011). Analyisis needs to be generally framed within the research questions in terms of the types of findings you are expecting. For example, one group will be significantly higher than another group on the dependent variable as an outcome of the treatment or independent variable. Terminology will change because of the statistics that are used to answer the research questions.

In ESL research an example of a research question within a study that incorporates a treatment and a scored measure of language skills could be: "Significant differences in written English language scores will exist between a treatment group of first year university ESL students that receive access to an online story telling program, than first year university ESL students who participate in the standard program. It is predicted that the treatment group will score higher than the standard group". Fraenkal et al. (2011) suggest that directional research questions (e.g., one group higher or lower than another) can be riskier to present and should only be used when researchers are confident of the expected findings. Otherwise, non-directional (differences between the two groups will exist) research questions should be presented.

Matching a Research Design Methodology With Aims

Irrespective of the type of issue or idea the study will attempt to clarify, strong connections are required between the research aims and the design and methodology of the research. De Vaus (2001) has noted that design and methods are not the same and must be considered independently, but within the project, operate in unison. Decisions pertaining to characteristics of the sample, availability of resources, time to implement the project, and skills of the research team will influence the approaches that can be implemented within the project. Research in ESL is suitable to a variety of methods that operate within the different quantitative designs outlined earlier.

Knowledge of the general demographic characteristics of the sample prior to the study is important in relation to the capacity to undertake group comparisons based on factors such as age, gender, country of origin etc to ensure it is representativeness. For example, if the size of the groups to be contrasted is not relatively similar in relation to the independent variable a number of several important statistical comparisons cease to be viable. Early design phases of the project will substantiate the availability of resources. Experimental designs involving interventions or treatments can be costly, or require specific technical skills so the research team must take these types of factors into consideration before finalizing the project plan. Time constraints will affect whether the project can utilize a cross-sectional or a longitudinal methodology within a correlational or a causal-comparative design. Cross-sectional methods involve the collection of data from multiple groups within a single time period. Longitudinal methods require access to the same cohort of participants over an extended interval involving multiple phases of data collection (Lauer, 2004). Finally, quantitative designs necessitate specific skills from the within the research team which should be apparent or acquired over the course of the project. More complex causal or experimental designs typically utilize more advance statics and it is imperative that a member of the team has the knowledge to ensure the data is collected correctly, and their skills are sufficiently developed to effectively use these techniques.

Data Collection In EFL Research

Data collection in EFL research will require undertaking a series of important steps to ensure that the design is fully instigated and aims are achieved. In many areas of educational research, the setting in which the data is to be collected has a major influence on viable procedural strategies (e.g., primary school, university, language college). Researchers must also work through tasks associated with sampling procedures and participant recruitment. Selection of instruments and interventions will require close review to ensure applicability to the samples recruited. Finally, the processes and procedures used to formulate a sample and administer the measures or treatment will require thorough detailing to support the fluidity of the project as a piece of useful research.

Evaluating the Setting

Quantitative data collection necessitates that the setting must be capable of facilitating access to the targeted groups. This can be either on-site or in the case of survey research and on-line environment can be created. The research team will need to negotiate with those who mange the settings (or create the on-line space) that participant access, working spaces, and equipment are available. Interaction regarding organisational and participant (or parent) consents must be undertaken as a prerequisite to the data collection commencing.

Recruiting and Selecting the Sample

The sample is the set of individuals that the researchers involve in the specific data collection, whereas, the population is the set of individuals to whom findings could be generalized (Dornyei, 2007). Recruitment and selection of participants should be equitable within the limitations of the procedural elements of the study. Researchers may not exclude participants on the basis of gender, race, national origin, religion, creed, education, or socioeconomic status.

Dornyei (2007) suggested that the procedures associated with formulating a sample can be considered in two main groups that are probability sampling and non-probability sampling. Probability sampling can be complex and often challenging to implement in research in ESL. The main probability sampling strategies include random, stratified random, systematic and cluster. The approach commonly adopted in The ESL field is non-probability sampling, which necessitates the acceptance of a level of statistical error in facilitating the selection of a representative sample that can be recruited by the ordinary researcher. Procedures used regularly are quota sampling, dimensional sampling, snowball sampling and convenience sampling. Each of these procedures are often adopted because of the restraints that a research must operate within in educational settings. Participants are often targeted as a combination of the features that the individuals represent the target group, and are available to the research team. Interestingly, in line with this notion of availability and convenience, Dornyei proposed that determining the size of the sample should be considered in terms of not how large a sample should be but rather in terms of what is the minimum acceptable sample size that maintains the viability of the project.

Instruments and Interventions

Quantitative data collected in ESL research is more commonly derived from tests relating to language skills or course performance, or survey questionnaires that source information related to participant attributes or program characteristics. Less common is the implementation of a treatment or intervention to determine if it can serve as an agent of change.

Surveys and questionnaires. Developing and administering surveys and questionnaires is a very important data collection methodology within ESL research. The popularity of this approach is primarily due to the ease, adaptability, and generalizability with which it can be undertaken and results conveyed (Schutt, 2012). Griffee (2012) provides a clear overview of how the development and use of questionnaires in language research should be managed. Firstly, in terms of administration select from the options of paper and pencil, on-line, or via telephone. Secondly, format must be considered to ensure that the components of demographics, closed-ended items, and/or open-ended items are included. Open-ended items are typically multiple choice or Likert type response formats. In ESL research, many projects will use a group-administered survey completed by individual respondents assembled together. Response rate is less of an issue in the group setting because most group members will participate, however, a concern is the possibility that respondents will feel coerced to participate and may not answer questions honestly (Schutt, 2012).

A survey questionnaire should be designed as an integrated whole, with each question and section serving some clear purpose and complementing the others. A standard introductory statement should be included that highlights appreciation, describes the steps of the survey, and reinforces that the survey is not the same as a test. Schutt presents an excellent summary of the basic strategy for developing both survey items and structure.

> Questions must be worded carefully to avoid confusing respondents, encouraging a less-than-honest response, or triggering biases. Inclusion of "Don't know" choices and neutral responses may help, but the presence of such options also affects the distribution of answers. Open-ended questions can be used to determine the meaning that respondents attach to their answers. Answers to any survey questions may be affected by the questions that precede them in a questionnaire or interview schedule. (p. 183)

Overall, when the research team decides to utilise a survey instrument for data collection they must also determine if existing measures with substantiated reliability and validity exist that meet the aims of the project, or there is the need to develop a new measure. If the latter is the case, researchers will also need to follow expected psychometric protocols associated with instrument development such as reliability, content validity, and construct validity. Data collection through the use of surveys is generally effective when the measure represents a coherent and accurate representation of an aim of the project.

Interventions. The use of interventions in experimental studies in ESL can strengthen the quality of the research, particularly in relation to specific teaching activities, programs, curriculum changes, or textbooks that purport to increase educational achievement and success. By identifying and empirically evaluating what is viable and effective in the management of teaching and learning in ESL through trialling specific treatments or program changes, evidence is generated to support the broader community of ESL practice. Gill and Hahs-Vaughn (2010) further proposed that by:

> Determining the efficacy of an intervention on a local scale is not only practically useful—it can help one's day to day teaching—but it is also important for the broader research community in that it may reveal conditions under which the treatment X works or does not work as well (p. 25).

Experimental treatments are typically more successful when the intervention is grounded in strong substantive theory, when implementation of treatment remains fully committed to that theory, the research setting is well managed, and when intervention is consistent over its delivery. In many educational field experiments these conditions are not met. Because teaching and learning settings are often large, complex, social organizations with multiple programs, disputatious politics, and conflicting stakeholder goals, the fidelity of the treatment programs can be highly variable (Shadish, Cook, & Campbell, 2002). At the simplest level experimental interventions in ESL that are well designed and managed can make a contribution by simply probing whether an' intervention-as-implemented' makes a marginal improvement beyond other associated influences or variables. The generation of useful data as an outcome of interventions is only possible when a substantive effort is made by researchers to ensuring the quality of that treatment both prior to and during implementation.

Processes and Procedures

Adopting both ethical and viable processes and procedures in collecting data, is a critical component in addressing research questions or supporting hypotheses. Data gathering as previously discussed in this section incorporates consideration about what variables to investigate, the unit of measurements, participants of the study (population and sample), participant protections, procedures used for selecting participants, the methods and procedures used for data collection, and any reliability or validity of collection methods (Cresswell, 2004). Procedures do not necessarily occur independently of each other but should operate in a uniform and orchestrated manner. For example, recruiting participants and decisions associated with the measures or treatments of the research can and, possibly should happen in unison. Although, many of the procedures of research require different attributes (e.g., communication skills, statistical knowledge, academic acumen), good quantitative researchers are capable of establishing procedural frameworks that demonstrate a logical and integrated sequence of formulating, implementing, and finalising the essential tasks of their investigation.

Quantitative research in ESL should also be bound by these expectations of quality practice

Data Analysis in EFL Research

The purpose of this section is to provide a general but brief overview of the main types of quantitative statistics that could be adopted in ESL research. Interestingly, the types of statistics used in educational research have remained relatively consistent and tend to represent the simpler end of the complexity continuum (Karadag, 2010). An essential preparatory phase in data analysis is to ensure that following collection the data is coded, entered, screened and cleaned (Dörnyei, 2007). Data analysis will be considered within the categories of descriptive statistics (including correlation), inferential statistics, construct statistics, and model testing statistics.

Descriptive Statistics

All quantitative research requires the reporting of basic descriptive statistics. Descriptive statistics constitute the basis of all quantitative analysis and its contribution must not be overlooked because advanced statistics are also used in the investigation (Karada., 2010). The role of descriptive statistics is to summarize sets of numerical data in order to present a concise simple overview of the trends and patterns of the data (Dörnyei, 2007). Data when considered as variables can be classified as numerical, non-numerical, discrete, categorical, nominal, ordinal, interval scale, and continuous. The main univariate statistics reported should be considered within the three categories of distribution, central tendency, and dispersion (Trochim, 2006). The details of information provided for these statistics are based upon descriptions by Ary et al. (2006) and McDonough & McDonough, (1997).

Distribution. The distribution is a summary of the frequency or occurrence of individual values or ranges of values for a variable. It is a considered as a representation of the layout of the data by highlighting where scores occurred and how the data is spread. For example, the distribution of gender composition at different year levels of an ESL course, or numbers of individuals who score at different grading values for a particular test. The two main presentation formats are tables that detail the percentage or number of occurrences for a variable and formulated categories (e.g., nationality, age group) and a frequency distribution chart such as histogram or line graph that presents a figure format of the data pattern.

Central tendency. The central tendency of a data set is an estimate of the "center" of the distribution of values. The three major types of estimates of central tendency are mean, median, and mode. The mean is the average of all scores from the sample; the median is the middle score of the range of the set of scores; and the mode is the score that occurs most frequently within the set of scores. An example of how central tendency data is shown is a set of 20 grammar test results in which 10 questions of 1 mark each were asked, and descriptive results indicated the mean was 6.6, the median was 7, and the mode was 6.

Dispersion. Spread of scores or dispersion of scores is typically reported as range, standard deviation and relative position. The range is basically the detail associated with the lowest and the highest score of the set of scores, and is calculated by subtracting the low score from the high score and adding one. Standard deviation measures how much on average individual scores of a given group vary or deviate from the mean score for this same group, or the average of the differences of scores from the mean. The main statistics that demonstrate relative position or where a score lies in relation to the other scores in the sample are z score, stanines, and percentile rank. A z score is defined as an indication of positive or negative difference above or below the mean. Stanine scores are a system of detailing Z scores in a format from 1-9 rather than negative to positive. A percentile rank indicates the percentage of scores from the set of scores that are above or below a given scores. If we consider the test example provided for central tendency, the range was 6, the standard deviation was 1.37, the z score spread was -2.2 to +2.2. In terms of percentile, if we refer to a score of 6, then 35 per cent of scores were at or below this score and 65 percent were above.

Descriptive statistics constitute a necessary and important element of the analysis procedure within the quantitative approach. The resultant data not only provides the basis for additional complex analyses, but just as importantly generates statistical information for the researcher to make judgements on the trends and patterns observed. For example, in a study examining final test scores of students completing EFL programs delivered in their country of origin compared with those who complete the program in a country where the first language is English, descriptive statistics allow the researcher to make initial commentary on how the trends pertaining to subgroups might generally differ. This could be illustrated through contrasts such as women may be performing better than men locally, older participants scoring lower when away from their country of origin, individuals with multiple language backgrounds score highest overall etc. In general, descriptive data serves as the succinct commencement point in considering how the data could be further explored or broadly communicated. The reporting of descriptive results also regularly utilises presentation formats such as tables, charts, and graphs as an illustrative framework for detailing trends and general contrasts.

Inferential Statistics

Inferential statistics are associated with formulating predictions or inferences about a population from observations and contrasts of sample data. These analyses utilise tools that allow researchers to estimate a level of confidence in inferences "that phenomena observed in samples will also appear in the populations from which the samples were drawn" (Ary et al., 2006, p. 210). Inferential results extend on the trends generated within descriptive findings by determining if differences between groups or test occasions are statistically significant. Statistical significance represents the likelihood that a result or relationship observed in a sample is caused by something other than random chance and therefore generalizable to the whole population (Dörnyei, 2007). Statistical hypothesis testing is employed to determine if a result is statistically significant or not and provides a "p-value" representing the probability that random chance could explain the result. A figure of a 5% or lower p-value is considered to be statistically significant.

The main set of basic inferential statistics includes t-tests, Analysis of Variance (ANOVA), Chi-square test, and correlation. The t-test procedure is used to compare two groups or a pair of repeated scores from a single group (e.g., males and females, semester one exam and semester exam). ANOVA is a similar contrast that is used when there a more than two groups or repetitions of a score to compare (e.g., low, middle, high income groups; language skill scores before, during, and after course completion). Chi-square analysis involves the examination of differences between proportions or frequencies of nominal or categorical data (e.g., yes or no scores contrasted with country of origin). The correlation procedure considers the relationship between variables, scores, or categories rather than the differences between the values. Results of correlational analysis provide an indication of the strength and direction of the association between scores or variables (e.g., strong positive relationship between years of previous English language experience and EFL course performance).

Advanced inferential statistical procedures include Multi-level analysis of variance (MANOVA), Analysis of co-variance (ANCOVA), and regression. MANOVA is a group comparison technique that examines multiple variables and multiple groups. The procedure could be implemented in an investigation of English reading and writing skill scores for EFL course students and contrasted against gender or year level in the program. Application of ANCOVA analysis is undertaken when the researcher is aware that differences in scores on a variable of interest exist prior to the implementation of a treatment. For example, students from a range of countries of origin are completing an on-line English language skills enhancement program. The researcher is interested in the efficacy of the program in improvement written English skills. It was observed that the pre-treatment scores varied substantially between cohorts according to their first language background. The ANCOVA procedure controls for these differences to ensure that post test comparisons are a consideration of the effect of the training program and not simply the influence of pre-treatment written English skills. Regression analyses are an extension of correlation that involve the examination of the relationship between multiple variables. The technique determines the capacity of one variable or scores to predict the scores on subsequent variables or scores. For example, a regression analysis could be used to evaluate if the selection exam for an EFL studies program is more effective in predicting scores on the final year written exam or students' scores on the National English language skills test.

Construct and Modelling Analysis

The process of data collection in EFL research will often involve the development and use of measures that are designed to assess a construct or set of attributes to represent that construct. Further to this, researchers will on occasions formulate studies that attempt to determine the mediating influence or linked association of one score or variable on others measured at a similar time or within a predetermined sequence. These outcomes can often be achieved through the use of statistical procedures associated with factor analysis and structural equation modelling.

The two main forms of factor analyses are Exploratory Factor Analysis (EFA) and Confirmatory Factor Analysis (CFA). Both forms as used to determine the factors that items within a questionnaire or survey could represent. In general, EFA is used when the researcher has developed a measure and serves to provide an indication of which items group together to form factors. Factors are considered to be linked to the construct on which the development of the measure was based. For example, in EFL research if a measure was developed to determine how students perceive the importance of their overall set of English skills (i.e., reading, writing, communicating) it can be analysed to ascertain if these domains around which the items were based exist as factors or are grouped in another pattern. If all the items related to reading, writing, and communicating skills group together, respectively, the measure could be considered to demonstrate a level of logical coherence. In subsequent studies in using the measure with different EFL populations, researchers could utilise CFA to evaluate that the factors proposed as an outcome of the EFA can be identified as an a priori model of the construct and factors of the measure. The use of both EFA and CFA are critical in the establishing the validity and viability of both newly developed and existing measures.

Structural Equation Modelling (SEM) is a statistical technique that allows investigators to consider a hypothesised model of relationships between variables of interest to their research question. The researcher constructs an a priori model, or path diagram, of possible associations and then uses the SEM to test the adequacy of the fit of these variables. For example, a project could be undertaken in which a path model is constructed to consider the predictive capacity of English language skills score, high school performance, and frequency of international travel on undergraduate performance in an ESL course. This score could then be linked with further study score performance at the post-graduate level, and then considered against relationships with post-graduate outcomes such as published output, scholarship application success, and ESL teaching opportunities (see Figure 1). This path model can also be evaluated on the basis on mediation effects of demographic variables such as age or gender. The broader aim of SEM and path analysis is to work towards the incorporation of available data to support or refute hypotheses associated with areas of interest to the field. For more in depth overviews of SEM and path analysis please see Hair, Black, Babin, and Anderson (2010) and Tabachnick and Fidell (2001).

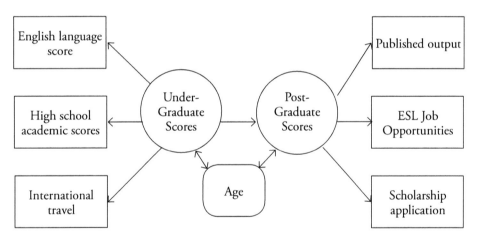

Figure 6.1 Hypothesised model of Post-graduate success in EFL studies (Tabachnick & Fidell, 2001)

Data Interpretation and Reporting

A critical phase in the quantitative research process is the interpretation and reporting of findings. It is accepted that a specific approach for detailing numerical results is required, generally involving the adoption of a pre-defined manuscript presentation design and a set of statistical styles as outlined in procedural texts for academic publishing such as the American Psychological Association (APA) publication manual (American Psychological Association, 2009) or the reporting chapter of Dornyei (2007). The typical elements of a quantitative research report adopting APA style include: Title page, Abstract, Introduction, Method, Results, Discussion, and References. As a broad guide to framing interpretation and reporting phase of a research project this section of the chapter will cover the following themes of results as numbers, contextualizing the numbers, and establishing meaning from the findings.

Numbers as Results

Quantitative statistics as described in previous sections of this chapter are first reported in a numerical context. The researcher should describe the patterns of descriptive data and outcomes of inferential and modeling analyses in a manner that accurately reflect the data, and strictly follow the underlying assumptions of the statistical procedures utilized. The results section need only present the information that will be absorbed into later discussion. If findings are detailed in a table then there is no need to repeat that information in the text, unless that information extends or refines the table results (Dornyei, 2007). A blend of precision and brevity should be an aim in the formulation of the results section. The detail contained within the numbers is important, and readers with basic experience in quantitative analysis should be able to work from that information. There is little need to extend numerical descriptors pertaining to the analyses into a text based overview of what the numbers already reveal. For example, if the analysis is related to a comparison of two groups on several variables associated with English skills, then in a results section focus on a table of resultant data and briefly summarize any required inferential detail related to significant group differences. I recommended "The Owl at Purdue Writing Lab" as an excellent site to guide both structuring of results and how this is integrated into the manuscript (Purdue Owl, 2014).

Contextualizing the Numbers

Descriptions of quantitative information should be focused on locating the resultant data relative to the research questions, and as a representation of the population of interest. McDonough and McDonough (1997) have proposed in relation to EFL research that "the researcher has to go back to the design and purpose of the research to decide what the result actually means" (p. 115). For example, a set of exam results in which the average score is very high could indicate that either the test is too easy or that the teaching was of exceptional quality and the students mastered the topic content. Depending on the possible reason for considering test scores as data, such as to determine the qualities of a new teaching technique, or two compare course performances of males and females then a high score as a result would have contrasting meanings. As an outcome of a new teaching technique this would be a very pleasing result, whereas in identifying possible differences between males and females it would add limited new information.

In considering and interpreting inferential results, attention should be directed toward the meaning of both significant and non-significant results. Using the example of pre-requisite skills that might contribute toward end of course results in an EFL program of studies, significant differences between groups classified on the basis of how many additional languages they speak could be influential in establishing selection criteria for courses (i.e. speaks more than two languages). In contrast, no differences between course outcome results when programs are delivered on-line or on-site could serve as evidence to administrators that off-campus teaching is equally as effective as face to face delivery.

Overall, it is essential in quantitative reporting that the numbers do not hide the meaning from all but those who have higher order statistical knowledge (Lazaraton, 2005). When the results are considered by the reader, the complexity of the presentation should not operate as a deterrent to those individuals with an interest in the research questions and context but are restricted in interpretation by a limited quantitative history. The framing and presentation of the numbers and the statistics in that manner may lead to the reader to not fully engage in the discussion sections of the manuscript.

Establishing Meaning

The final phase in the quantitative data collection and reporting process is to ensure that details regarding numerical and statistical patterns are interpreted in relation to existing research, and receive logical consideration on the part of the researcher. Statistical patterns generated as an outcome of any investigation cannot exist in isolation, and must be framed against the results reported in similar studies, connected to relevant theory, and coherently linked with the original research questions. If a researcher is interested in determining if linguistics progression rates of students located in Asia demonstrate any discriminating characteristics then these findings need to be considered in relation to similar studies in Asia but also investigations based in Europe and first language English speaking countries. Highlighting the contrasts and similarities in the patterns observed with earlier research, and considering the associations the other researchers have proposed in relation to theory will facilitate a framework to support the implications drawn in relation any new research. The consideration of the research questions is best managed when the logical inference perceived as an outcome of the descriptive and inferential analyses is clearly linked with current and established ideas accepted within the EFL research domain.

Overall, findings can most effectively generate a rationality of meaning when the researcher and the readers share, and acknowledge (not necessarily accept), matching or comparable assumptions (Chu, N.D.). It is critical that the manuscript or report serves as the primary source to explain your assumptions and how these connect to your data and findings. When the quantitative research project is framed upon a solid theoretical foundation it facilitates greater opportunity to generalize your findings. Chu proposed a simple but accurate point to be conscious of in reporting your research in that "as you extrapolate or generalize, you must examine your assumptions in order not to exceed the boundaries of your framework or the quality of your data". (see http://digitalcommons.unl.edu/libphilprac/advice.html).

Summary

Highlighting the perceived advantages of the quantitative analyses methodology such as precise conceptualization and measurement, sophisticated statistical analyses, and defined reporting procedures (Voils, Sandelowski, Barroso, & Hasselblad, 2008) may serve as a stimulus for new researchers to consider this approach. However, these advantages will only be of benefit if the researcher is organized in the pre-data collection phases of the investigation. Deciding upon the type of design to be implemented and connecting this to the broader planning associated with the aims of the research is critical. Data collection procedures in relation to setting, sample, and instrumentation must be closely matched to the research design. For example, awareness of the requirements associated with intervention period and participant numbers (i.e., quasi-experimental), will necessitate different strategies than a large scale survey project in which correlational and descriptive data will be incorporated. Subsequent data analyses will be of greatest value when the original design and planning is strong. New researchers should seek as much information as possible regarding the wide variety of techniques that can be used to analyse the data after collection. Although current analysis software provides ample opportunity for the researcher to perform a variety of descriptive, inferential, construct, and modelling analyses, it is recommended that the researcher must be confident that they can accurately interpret the resultant output. Finally, irrespective of design, procedure, and analysis, results of any study in the EFL will only be of value when interpretation is coherent and located within the broader body of literature that the research community supports.

Dr. Anthony Watt
College of Education
Victoria University, Australia

References

American Psychological Association. (2009). *Publication manual of the American Psychological Association* (6th ed.). Washington, DC: American Psychological Association.

Ary, D., Jacobs, L. C., Razavieh, A., & Sorensen, C. (2006). *Introduction to research in education* (7th ed.). Belmont, CA: Thomson Wadsworth.

Anderman, E. (2003) *Research methods: An overview*. The Gale Group http://www.education.com/reference/article/research-methods-an-overview/

Berry, J. (2005). *Quantitative Methods in Education*. Research Centre for Teaching Mathematics, University of Plymouth. http://www.edu.plymouth.ac.uk/resined/quantitative/quanthme.htm

Brown, J. D. (2011). Quantitative research in second language studies. In E. Hinkel (Ed.), *Handbook of research on second language teaching and learning* (Vol. 2) (pp. 190-206). New York: Routledge.

Chu, F. T. (N.D.) *Factors you can control when writing a paper*. Malpass Library Western Illinois University. http://digitalcommons.unl.edu/libphilprac/advice.html

Creswell, J. W. (2004). *Educational research: Planning, conducting, and evaluating quantitative and qualitative research*, 2nd ed. Columbus, OH: Prentice Hall.

Cronbach, L. (1976). *Research on classrooms and schools: Formulation of questions, design and analysis.* Stanford Univ., Calif. Stanford Evaluation Consortium.

Crookes, G., & Lehner, A. (1998). Aspects of process in an ESL critical pedagogy teacher education course. *TESOL Quarterly*, 32(2), 319-328.

De Vaus, D. A. (2001). Research design in social research. London: SAGE.

Dimsdale, T., & Kutner, M. (2004). *Becoming an educated consumer of research: A quick look at the basics of research methodologies and design.* Meeting of the Minds Practitioner-Researcher Symposium. American Institutes for Research, Sacramento, CA.

Dörnyei, Z. (2007). *Research methods in applied linguistics: Quantitative, qualitative and mixed methodologies.* Oxford: Oxford University Press.

Fraenkel, J., Wallen, N. & Hyun (2011). *How to design and evaluate research in education.* New York: McGraw-Hill

Gall, M. D., Borg, W. R., Gall, J. P. (2003). *Educational research: An introduction.* (7th Edition). White Plains, New York: Longman.

Gay, L., Mills, G., & Airasian, P. (2006). *Educational research: Competencies for analysis and applications.* New Jersey: Pearson Education, Inc.

Gill, M. & Hahs-Vaughn, D. (2010). Does it work? A guide to investigating the efficacy of interventions in educational research. *Current Issues in Education*, 13(4), 1-32.

Griffee, Dale T. (2012). *An introduction to second language research methods: Design and data.* Berkeley, CA: TESL-EJ Publications.

Hair, J. F., Black, W. C., Babin, B. J., & Anderson, R. E. (2010). *Multivariate data analysis* (7th ed.).Upper Saddle River, NJ: Prentice-Hall.

Johnson, B. (2000). It's (beyond) time to drop the terms causal-comparative and correlational. Research in Education ITFORUM PAPER #43 http://itech1.coe.uga.edu/itforum/home.html

Karadağ, E. (2010). An analysis of research methods and statistical techniques used by doctoral dissertation at the education sciences in Turkey. *Current Issues in Education*, 13(4), 1-21.

Lauer, P. A. (2004). *Policymaker's primer on education research. How to understand, evaluate, and use it.* Aurora, CO: Midcontinent Research for Education and Learning (McREL) and Denver, CO: Education Commission of the States (ECS). Available from: www.ecs.org/researchprimer.

Lazaraton, A. (2005). Quantitative research methods. In E. Hinkel (Ed.), *Handbook of research in second language learning* (pp. 209-224). Mahwah, NJ: Lawrence Erlbaum.

McDonough, J. & S. McDonough. (1997). Principles and problems—what makes good research? *Research Methods for English Language Teachers.* Arnold: London.

McEwan, Patrick J. (2008). Quantitative research methods in education finance and policy. In Helen F. Ladd and Edward B. Fiske (Eds.) *Handbook of research in education finance and policy*, (pp. 87-104). New York: Routledge.

Purdue OWL (2014). *The writing lab & the OWL at Purdue.* Purdue University. https://owl. english. purdue.edu/owl/ retrieved Jan 2014.

Schutt, Russell K. 2012. *Investigating the social world: The process and practice of research*, 7th ed. Thousand Oaks, CA: SAGE Publications.

Shadish, W.R., Cook, T.D., & Campbell, D.T. (2002). *Experimental and quasi-experimental designs for generalized causal inference.* Boston: Houghton-Mifflin.

Tabachnick, B. G., & Fidell, L. S. (2001). *Using multivariate statistics* (4th ed.). Needham Heights, MA: Allyn & Bacon.

Trochim, W.M. (2006) *The research methods knowledge base*, 2nd Edition. http://www.social. researchmethods.net/kb/ Retrieved May, 2013.

Voils, C.I., Sandelowski, M., Barroso, J., & Hasselblad, V. (2008). Making sense of qualitative and quantitative findings in mixed research synthesis studies. *Field Methods*, 20 (1), 3-25.

Chapter Seven

Making 'Work' Matter

The Praxis of Collecting and Analysing Data

NAOKO ARAKI AND KIM SENIOR

Researching in EFL classrooms is complicated and challenged by a number of factors: the position of English as a global language; global mobility and its impact on cultural identity; the call for greater communicative competencies in EFL learners; proliferation of innovative pedagogical repertoires in EFL teaching; as well as the demands of teacher accountability in relation to student performance. As an interface between global change and national aspiration, EFL classrooms are sites of competing priorities and expectations. The authors encourage teacher/researchers wishing to explore and understand such environments to consider ways of research that make the most of 'work' by all involved (teachers, students, school staff and community). In our experience, reconsidering beyond the binaries of what counts as work/research, what is data/analysis and blurring the lines between meaning/interpretation have proven to be a pragmatic and productive space in the EFL context. Through the illustration of one of our research projects, we theorise that by making the work of PELT 'matter', thresholds to deeper and nuanced understandings of language learning and teaching are possible.

M. Vicars et al. (eds.), *The Praxis of English Language Teaching and Learning (PELT)*, 115–140.

Setting the Scene

The authors are both teachers of additional languages: teaching English as an additional language in Japan and Australia as well as teaching Japanese as an additional language in Australia. Both authors have been additional language students; between us we bring extensive intercultural experience as learners and teachers to our role as educational researchers. In this chapter we take the methodological positioning of practitioner researchers concerned with balancing inherent issues of reflexivity with those of a critical understanding of classroom praxis. Specifically we are interested in how language teacher/researchers might 'see' the world of the classroom differently in order to explore the junctures of theory, practice and learning. We discuss our work in this chapter to:

- emphasise the productive or generative nature of data and analysis;

- bring about 'an immediate change agenda at its heart' (Thomson, 2008, p 7) when working with participants in a research process;

- embrace the contradictions, contrary and confounding within classroom research as opportunities not liabilities;

- explore and explicate innovative and responsive research approaches for communicative EFL classrooms; and

- bring a gestalt focus to the nature of learning and teaching for all involved in the research process.

Within EFL research literature it is common to encounter research *on* students; however when researching learners in classrooms, Thomson (2008) suggests researchers should consider how they could work *with* participants. Working with the research participants brings 'an immediate change agenda at its heart' (Thomson, 2008, p. 7). From the outset and during key critical points attention gravitates to the core foci and main pedagogical action of the research; researchers are drawn into events, episodes or encounters significant to all participants. In the role of co-researcher, students and teachers may speak of knowing and being within the learning experience and not just of the end product of such experience. We further suggest that working *alongside* peers and participants in a contemporaneous and deliberate way is attentive to a critical ontological practice.

By its very nature classroom research and, in particular, classroom research by practitioner researchers can be a logistical nightmare. A danger arises that our response may be to instill or seek order and certainty within an environment inherently unpredictable and chaotic. The researcher may select data collection and analysis methods that foregrounds individuality and specificity at the expense of the indivisibility of classroom pedagogy. Without carefully considering the implications of particular data sets limited and limiting research may be the end result. Ensuring that the *procedures* of research that are necessarily specific and rigorous need not proclude research that is attentive to the complexity of social reality and human experience. Earlier chapters have elaborated upon the field of EFL research and critical pedagogy as well as research practices (narrative, critical action research and arts-based approaches) that are significant to practitioners wishing to engage, or re-engage, with praxis and classroom-based research. Working with students and colleagues to gather and generate data is an authentic exercise, offering a dialogical space for EFL teachers and students to re-experience the classroom and learning as a site of knowledge production. We, the authors, propose that using analytical approaches that include all those involved in the EFL classroom disrupts hierarchical cultural and pedagogical relationships. In the following pages we put forward a range of evidence in narrative and visual form as a means to research praxis in the EFL environment.

Characters, Place and Time: A Working Field Narrative

It is a warm spring morning and sunlight brightens the third floor multi-purpose room of the school where I am to begin my first Drama-English lesson in Japan. The well-polished wooden floor makes it difficult to walk in the provided plastic slippers[1]. I cannot wait to take them off. There are foldable chairs at the side of the room and a blackboard located in the middle of the room. The room is spacious: perfect for Drama-English language activities with the Year Six students.

---

[1]   As a standard custom, students and teachers in Japanese schools take their shoes off at the entry of the school and wear inside shoes or slippers. Guests and visitors are also expected to wear supplied slippers while inside the school buildings.

As the bell sounds to indicate the first period has concluded, cheerful voices suddenly can be heard from the end of the corridor. I quickly finish setting up for this very first lesson. There is only 5 minutes left before they come to this room—my room. Even though the second period bell has not yet sounded, the first class of Year Six students enter very quietly in two straight lines; one line boys and the other girls. They appear to be very well disciplined and endlessly troop into the room: there are thirty-five students altogether in this one class. All the students are wearing school regulation inside-shoes, but no school uniform. The girls wear red inside shoes and the boys, blue. With a watchful eye on his students, and without a welcoming smile on his face, the classroom teacher accompanies his charges. Childhood memories from my own Japanese school flash to mind.

I feel myself getting increasingly nervous about the lesson and I experience a rush of emotions. I am in Year 6 class again with that old grumpy unexpressive teacher. All sorts of memories about the Japanese schools I attended occupy my thoughts punctuated by the faces of long forgotten classmates. Bringing myself to the present I smile and welcome them all with a cheery "Hello!"

"あの、どこに座らせればいいですか。 *(Excuse me. How would you want my students to sit?)" asks Tanaka sensei, the Year 6 classroom teacher, who I've never met before.*

I try a broader smile and reply, "どこでもいいですよ、、、この辺で。 *(Anywhere they like. -Around here is fine)."*

"どこでもって、、、 *(Anywhere they like!?)"*

After an audible sigh, "じゃあ、教室と同じように座って。早く静かに行動。 *(Alright everyone, sit in the same seating order as the classroom. Get into your positions quickly without talking)."*

His sigh reminds me that I am dealing with students and teachers in Japan, not Australia. I'd forgotten that Japanese students expect teachers to provide very detailed instructions and direction. Obviously Tanaka sensei values that kind of approach in his practice and I wonder nervously how long it will take for me to develop a rapport with his students. My intent is to offer them the opportunity to make a number of personal choices. They will be making many decisions by themselves in this Drama-English class, which may very well differ from Tanaka sensei's style. They will be taking charge of their learning. I am looking for active participation. The students start dispersing into smaller han[2] groups. One leader in each group turn to face the other group members and in unison starts giving commands:

"前にならえ！ *(Line up!)*"

The leaders place their hands on their hips and other children in the line face them and raise their arms to shoulder height in line with the shoulders of the child in front without touching. Once the lines become straight, the group is commanded to sit. The students wait for my lesson to start: seated, quiet, clasping their knees with their hands. (Araki 2005, translated research journal entry)

The above data fragment depicts one moment during the first meeting between a Year 6 English as a foreign language (EFL) class and a teacher/researcher in Japan. It represents the researcher's responses to the first day back in a Japanese school after an absence of ten years. She had forgotten about the routine way lessons in a Japanese school are run as well as the different expectations of students and teachers. She had also forgotten how, even in the past, some of these practices rankled her. In the moment following that one sigh, she made a mental note to come back and think about those reactions and exchanges. As an 'empathetic outsider' (Somekh 1995, p.241) Araki accepted the important role that Tanaka sensei's cooperation and participation would play in the success or otherwise of her Drama-English program. She also held hopes that Tanaka sensei and his students would join her in a research project to investigate: 'How do students respond to drama based EFL learning?' and 'How do colleagues with differing EFL skills and experience work collaboratively within an action research environment?' With only six months set aside for the Drama-English program, to be conducted across three Year 6 classes in one primary school, Araki was eager to create an inviting and collegial environment from the beginning. This Drama-English program (Araki 2006) is documented in greater detail elsewhere but for the purposes of this chapter the authors will concentrate on how data and data analysis was productively put to work through certain interludes during the research project. Our intent is not to be exhaustive in our illustration but rather to theorise some of the provocations and speculations brought to light during this particular project.

---

2   Gender-mixed groups of six used in most Japanese schools.

Did the characters, events, actions or points of view in the narrative remind you of a story or scene that you have experienced in a classroom or with a colleague? Did the narrative provoke you to ask questions or formulate ideas as to why the scene played out the way it did? By utilizing central components of narrative: employment, character, scene, place, time and point-of-view (Clandinin & Connelly 2000, p.26) even the briefest fragment of a field text offers rich data for critical inquiry into the praxis of English learning and teaching (PELT). Reader response to, and writer reflection upon, data provides thresholds to interpretation and analysis. As Chase (2011) describes, narrative inquiry itself is:

'a distinct form of discourse: as meaning making through the shaping or ordering of experience, a way of understanding one's own or others' actions, of organizing events and objects into a meaningful whole, of connecting and seeing the consequences of actions and events over time' (p 421).

We argue that the capacity of narrative data to generate multiple interpretations affords a rich dialogical and recursive approach to classroom research. Further, the significant place of visual data as a catalyst for interpretative and representative data in this particular classroom research project is outlined.

Data and Data Analysis

Making Teaching and Researching Work Matter

The range of data available to researchers is extensive. O'Toole and Beckett (2009) conveniently categorise three forms of data: participant, documenting and experimental. Interviews and questionnaires are examples of participant data that are widely called upon in research, but perhaps are under utilized. Keegan (2009) asserts that interviews involve an ethnographic element 'watching people's behavior, how they express themselves, how they respond in the particular situation, how they interact with the moderator and other participants' (p. 102). The ethnographic elements, or components, of expression, response and interaction can play a role in generating data. In classroom based pedagogical research generating such data crystalizes the underlying complexities of any given exchange. Returning to the events that opened this chapter and that audible sigh, the following narrative is Araki's later exploration of the events working from Tanaka sensei's perspective:

I have been teaching over twenty years. A few days ago the principal informed all Year 6 teachers that a researcher from an Australian university was coming to demonstrate EFL curriculum using drama conventions. I don't know anything about drama! The only 'drama' I can think of is Kabuki or those TV soaps. Will she make my students perform on a stage in English!? My students are not good at English at all. They really only start learning English as an academic subject next year in junior high school. They can only say 'Hello', but that is about all.

I know the Ministry of Education will be officially introducing English in primary schools soon... but I chose to become a primary school teacher because I wouldn't have to teach English. And all Year 5 and 6 classroom teachers are appointed to teach English, but we are not EFL specialists. This new direction is really concerning. I have no real say. I guess I will have to go along with it until I retire. This Australian researcher is apparently a Japanese person who has been teaching in Australian schools and is willing to teach English to all Year 6 students every week for the next three months. All Year 6 teachers, including myself, are experienced teachers but we are not confident in teaching English. I know my pronunciation is terrible. How can I teach English with this terrible pronunciation and strong accent? One of my students just came back from overseas after spending two years at a local school. His pronunciation is much better than mine. So, in a way, I welcome some ideas about how we can teach English....

Today is the day that the researcher will be taking my students for the very first time. I had better prepare my students for this new class, but none of us teachers have met her before or know anything about her really. Only the vice principal and principal have met her several times and discussed this project. I did manage to say to my students before the class, 'We have a special guest today who will teach English. Remember to behave and follow my instructions without any chatter. You are all Year 6 students. I expect you to be on your best behavior in front of this guest. Han leaders, make sure that you group is lined up straight. We need to be in a multi purpose room before the bell goes. Hurry up, now.'

When we arrived at the room, I was very surprised to see a young Japanese woman standing by the blackboard setting up a CD player. What can she teach? She looks so young, and <u>she</u> is a researcher? Oh, she greeted us in English... This *is Japan. What does she expect me to say? I am not here to learn English! I am going to use Japanese.*

My students were a bit nervous but the first lesson went OK. They seemed to enjoy the guest teacher, although the lesson was very different from what I expected. I thought she would teach some target vocabulary and get my class repeat after her. And perhaps do some English language games. The lesson was all in English with a lot of movement about the room. At least the students got some physical exercise; but I was a bit taken back that the she didn't seem to know how classes should be run. Is she really Japanese? In the beginning when I asked her where and how she wanted the students seated, she vaguely indicated 'somewhere around here'. I found that a bit irresponsible, how did she expect to establish a disciplined beginning to this new class? When I think about it she didn't give clear instructions to prepare the students for listening either! Learning cannot start until students are sitting nicely in a row with straight posture. They cannot just sit anyhow and anywhere they like! (Araki 2005, translated research journal entry)

The narrative above was constructed by Araki bringing a range of data sets together in relation to Tanaka sensei's responses to the Drama-English teaching approach and program. Data included her research journals and observation notes, his response to written questionnaires and semi-structured interviews, as well as dialogue captured during video-taping of classes. All questionnaires and formal semi-structured interviews were conducted at the conclusion of the project in Japanese. All Year 6 teachers initially responded to the written questionnaires and follow up interviews were conducted elaborating and clarifying individual views and opinions. In this way, conducting questionnaires and interviews after the project gave Araki ample of time to develop a rapport with her participants in what she knew would be a culturally and professionally sensitive environment. Towards the end of the project, Tanaka sensei welcomed some of the drama-based tasks as he could see how they might also be relevant in the way he could teach history. This opening in Tanaka's interest in drama-based EFL pedagogy allowed an incisive professional yet collegial dialogue to develop. Araki began to see a complex picture emerge of an experienced teacher deeply invested in the responsibility for his students learning, open to new pedagogical approaches but also a vulnerable individual. In the interviews Tanaka sensei's initial reserved enthusiasm to the project was coloured by a complex mix of national language policy changes, leadership expectations, school community aspirations, and his own feelings of inadequacy as an EFL learner, let alone an EFL teacher. Further, the video-taped classes provided additional insight into the gradual changes in Tanaka sensei's participation and interaction in the English classes.

Photographs, video-recording, field notes/research log, journals or reflective notes are documenting data. O'Toole and Beckett (2009) warn that with regard to writing reflective journals new researchers tend ' just to describe what happened in a simple narrative of the explicit action, or to dive into unstructured stream-of-consciousness personal feelings about the experience' (p. 124). They suggest inviting participants to contribute in some way to the journaling process in a purposeful manner (such as writing responses to specific questions or prompts) as a means of enriching the reflective nature of the research journal. Field notes and reflective journals can be written in a narrative form detailing atmosphere, significant events, participants' interactions, and/or emotions. Categorising various forms of data as participant data, documenting data, and experimental data can be useful but it is imperative to remember that this is simply for convenience. Data sets may overlap or can be multi-functional: in fact, the authors suggest that making data 'work' in this way is more productive. To make the most of what you have as a researcher makes greater sense than to burden yourself and your participants with the intrusion of too many data instruments and an inevitable over-indulgence of raw data.

When designing data collection in EFL, it needs to be kept in mind the importance of endeavouring to capture the complexities of teaching and learning with its multitude of interactions within the research site. An interesting factor that arose from Araki's research was the matter of working within a research site that moved between English and Japanese. The EFL classes were conducted in English but the classroom was punctuated by comments or interaction in mother tongue. Araki found herself 'teaching' in English and simultaneously 'researching' in Japanese: giving instructions to the class in Japanese, doing actual drama based EFL activities with the students in English; thinking in Japanese and English while speaking to her participant teachers in Japanese; and reminiscing in both Japanese and English. Her research journal and field notes were often a mixture of both languages.

The choice of language for data collection and the matter of translation itself are generally considered ethical issues. We contend that the slippage and interplay between languages is another fecund source of theorizing in EFL research. Including the participants' first language in a research process allows researchers to investigate valuable cultural and relational data circulating a socio-linguistic research site. The simple verbal exchange between Araki and Tanaka sensei upon their first meeting would seem pedestrian in its English translation; however the Japanese hints at something deeper at work. Japanese language has particular forms of polite language (*Keigo* and *Teineigo*) these levels of politeness differ according to specific contexts; factors such as the gender, age and social position of those speaking determines the level of language to be used. Conversely, these levels of politeness may also be used by the speaker to determine the context of the exchange—to emphasise difference in gender, age or social position. Araki kept an explicit level of politeness through out the project with all the Year 6 teachers, she was aware of her position as a young, female outsider despite being a fully qualified and experience EFL teacher. Tanaka sensei began his interactions with Araki using a minimal level of polite language, however there was a documented change in this as the program progressed. By the concluding interviews he was not only more garrulous he was also less attentive to the strictures of *Teineigo*. This significant change and shift in professional regard was clearly recorded in the 'Japanese' data but could easily have been overlooked. Like the opening narrative field note of this chapter, the significant initial exchange between Araki and Tanaka sensei can be easily incorporated into the text. If their responses are relatively short, it can be included in the paragraph, or the use of footnotes is also useful for longer sentences and additional explanations for specific cultural and pedagogical contexts.

When considering how to work *with* the Year 6 students as participants to her research Araki was aware she was an 'outsider' (albeit an honoured guest) who had to make conscious pedagogical decisions to gain some level of mutual trust. Despite being a non-native EFL teacher Araki was concerned that students' could bring with them a high level of anxiety in what is generally regarded as a high stakes subject in Japan. She was also aware that the drama-based communicative approach could be asking the students to work in an unfamiliar way with language and language learning. Working responsively with student interests, work required of the EFL class as well as her own research work, Araki used drawing as a familiar and joyful task to 'listen' and engage with the students. Varga-Atkins and O'Brien (2009) argue that drawings turn 'the dual interview into a 'three-way' process where the drawing tool acted as stimulus for the interviewer. It also became the record of the discussion and a further source for elaboration and questioning' (p. 53). Araki found this particularly useful to her research context; students that would otherwise have remained dutifully silent or respectfully acquiescent opened up a discussion about their learning through this process as well as providing valuable documenting data.

Fig. 7.1: Student drawing response to the 'Hungry Caterpillar' Drama-English class activity

The image above visually evidences and documents how one young Year 6 participant in the Drama-English program came to understand an unfamiliar prepositional concept. The word 'through' is considered advanced vocabulary for Japanese Year 6 students as there is no equivalent preposition in Japanese. As a means of introducing the use of prepositions, including 'through', Araki invited students to became a tiny caterpillar who went looking for food in EFL drama pedagogy activities. In this drama activity students moved around the classroom pretending to be a caterpillars consuming all sorts of fresh or processed foods in varying states of decay; they moved like caterpillars on the floor physically imaging the world from a caterpillars perspective. Using their experiences in the classroom (solely conducted in English) around this topic Araki asked students to use inspiration from the drama based EFL classes to draw the world from a tiny caterpillar's perspective. She gave instructions for this drawing task in Japanese. They were given an open invitation to draw whatever food their particular caterpillar ate, how much, when and where it was eaten. The only language requirement for the task was to label the food in English and write the day of the week it was consumed. The use of a bilingual dictionary was encouraged in this activity to develop their learning strategy.

Araki was curious to find out how the caterpillar activity in their EFL class may effect or affect student learning. She was also aware that 'Image-making provides an opportunity to represent experience, a tangible process and product, within which stories are inherent, or out of which stories are (re)created' (Leitch, 2008:39). The grape drawing clearly evidenced this student was able to picture in her mind what 'through' meant and in an exchange with Araki about her drawing, she was able to elaborate and verbalise the concept in simple English.

The authors of this chapter recognise a great potential in the use of drawings for EFL learners and EFL practitioner researchers. The caterpillar drawing exercise was a deliberate part of data collection in this project. Araki embedded the exercise within the interview process; she had a dual purpose for the drawing task. In the first instance, drawing was a creative and nonthreatening way for the students to confidently represent their caterpillar world and expressing themselves in English. Secondly, these products of both learning and artistic expression in turn became a catalyst for dialog between Araki and her co-participants as 'source for elaboration and questioning' (Varga-Atkins and O'Brien, 2009, p. 53). The students' drawing and writing work was purposeful, meaningful and valued data.

Using data and generating data with students is not only an authentic exercise, it offers a dialogical space for English language teachers and learners to re-experience and reflect upon learning in the classroom. The classroom becomes a site of knowledge production where student products are more than an illustration of learning but are centre pieces to discussion about 'our' teaching and learning.

Working collaboratively in this way with students and other teachers brings an attention to classroom relationships and the interdependent nature of teaching and learning. In a critical learning environment, narrative data is particularly useful 'to work collaboratively with research participants to improve the quality of their everyday experiences' (Chase, 2011 pp. 421-422). While, researchers need to consider data that will provide that most appropriate evidence for their research inquiry, this need not necessarily involve extra work. Making the work matter at many levels is pragmatic and can also have some unexpected consequences; the Year 6 students in Araki's study treasured their art-responses to such an extent that on their own initiative students collated the work to form their own hungry caterpillar book with the purpose to share with other students.

Data Analysis as Critical Work

Analytical work within the praxis environment is an opportunity for practitioner or 'empathetic' researchers to draw upon their pedagogical experience and understandings to *re-search* the classroom as a critical ontological site. Kincheloe (2011) delineates twenty three ideas on the notion of Critical Ontology for teachers, four of these are of particular relevance to researching critically in EFL classroom:

- "to appreciate the autopoietic (self-producing) aspect of the "self" in order to gain a more sophisticated capacity to reshape our lives";

- "to conceptualize new ways of analyzing experience and apply it to the reconstruction of selfhood";

- "to become detectives of difference who search for new ways of being human"; and

- "to conceptualize the emergent self as virtual; this means that depending on its relationships it is always capable of change and has no essential central controlling mechanism" (pp. 202-203).

We discuss these in terms of working with or alongside our co-researchers since we are deeply committed to the importance of making 'work' matter. Kincheloe's first point speaks to sophistication—urging practitioner researchers to resist the seduction of simplification or quick answers and not just point out complexity but work with it. In the EFL context, and particularly with an eye to the issues we raised in the introduction to this chapter, researchers must devise ways to work with the self-producing. Some researchers such as Vadeboncoeur (1998 cited in Le Compte 2010) approach the analytical analysis of attitudinal change to innovative teaching program by sorting individual data sets (interviews, field notes and student journals); documenting emergent change at various stages of individual transformative consciousness. However, in Araki's project she wove her analysis from a variety of data sets. In both the illustrative field narratives at the beginning of this chapter and in later data sets related to Araki's research project, she sought to recognize her co-participants beyond stable subjective entities. She sought to generate critical analytical data that endeavours to understand participants might be reshaping their lives as intersubjective agents within pedagogical relationships. By bringing together individual data sets (field notes, reflective journals, semi-structured and informal interviews, visual images) into working narratives, the autopoietic appears as a complex relation of self, Other, place, time and environment.

This dialogical and recursive data process allows analysis to take place that challenges the 'central controlling mechanism' of the teacher/researcher as *Knower* or central authority in the classroom. As Antonia Darder (2002) clearly illustrates in her book the negotiation of power and authority even in an innovative classroom can easily default to traditional cultural values of reproduction. This also applies to EFL classrooms. Teachers, practitioner researchers and students tend to revert to their comfort zones, instead of exploring, constructing or re-constructing in the innovative space. New and experienced researchers at some stage might feel uncertainty or frustration regarding 'getting' or collecting rich and relevant data. We suggest that engaging in this creative dialogic representation of data presents an opportunity: a reflexive 'between' space to explore difference; conceptualisations of self in the making; and critical ontological enactment. In Araki's first narratives, the seemingly simple issue of where students are to sit becomes a complex exploration of understanding. It recognises the contexualised social structures and the interrelationship of power and authority at work between Tanaka sensei, Araki and the students. Kincheloe (2003 cited in Hayes et al, 2011) suggests that "teachers who understand this critical ontological process can use these notions to rethink their lives and their teacher persona... self-organize and reorganize the field to new levels of complexity where new patterns and processes allow us to rethink the nature of our being and the possibility of our becoming' (p 205). We would suggest the same applies, with even greater facility within the culturally and socio-linguistically rich EFL classroom. It applies to students' first and additional languages.

As we continue in this chapter to further make the work of both teachers and students matter, we assert that within this critical analysis process that not only do students have a capacity to contribute to inquiry or exploration of teaching and learning with the classroom, but they have a right to do so. Even if the groundwork for such a right is not present, or appears not to be present, the responsibility of those involved in the process is to provide opportunity for this to occur. In this respect, researching in the EFL environment becomes a doubled opportunity for teacher/student/researcher to engage in exploring ontological positioning whilst specifically working within the place of language and culture production and reproduction.

Data Analysis as Dialogic Work

The process of analysis is one of piecing together data, making the invisible apparent, deciding what is significant and insignificant, and linking seemingly unrelated facets of experience together. Analysis is a creative process of organizing data so that the analytic scheme will emerge. Texts are read multiple times in a hermeneutic circle, considering how the whole illuminates the parts, and how the parts in turn offer a fuller and more complex picture of the whole, which then leads to a better understanding of the parts (Josselson, 2011, p. 227).

Analysing qualitative data is a complex yet rewarding process, as collected data can be ambiguous and suggest a multiplicity of meanings. So while LeCompte (2010) suggests that 'the task of analysis…requires researchers first to determine how to organize their data and use it to construct an intact portrait of the original phenomenon under study and second, to tell readers what that portrait means' (p.147), this might not always be so straight forward. Engaging an analytical process that includes co-participants will necessarily involve renegotiation of accepted roles and responsibilities; disrupting usual patterns of teacher/researcher/student relationships will take time and need careful planning. It may not be appropriate for all collected data to be shared, ethical considerations will restrict access to research journals and personal interviews. Other data, such as student work, group interviews, or video or photo images may be shared with participants and become part of an ongoing discussion about what happened, why, or what it might mean. Instead of constructing a single portrait of the phenomenon at a single point in time, what becomes possible is a multifaceted or crystallized rendering of meaningful moments or incidents across a period of inquiry.

Researchers might experience a feeling of being lost in a 'maze' of such data but by talking their way out of the maze, divergent participant understandings and meanings may become apparent. Researchers need to spend some time wondering in, out, and between various data sets in order for 'data to speak directly' (O'Toole and Beckett, 2009, p. 171). In Araki's work with the Year 6 drama-based English classes, she created a discursive process whereby co-participants and specific data sets informed the evolving inquiry. Classroom discussions became sites for deliberation about what tasks or activities meant to students and how they were negotiating the teaching and learning in the drama-based EFL context. Araki, purposefully made space within the class to talk about and, more importantly, listen to what her co-particpants were telling her about their experience. Rather than a one off evaluative event, she encouraged a practice of pondering and reflective conversation in and outside the classes. Ellingson (2009) suggests nine wonderings in qualitative data analysis that may be useful in a complex environment such as an EFL classroom. We have interpreted three of these as specific catalysts for on going dialogic work:

- What cases, event, stories, or details come to mind immediately when [we] think about [our] data?

- How does [our pedagogical] identity relate to [our] work?

- What have my [co]participants taught me about their worlds? About mine? (p.75)

Never a neat process, analysis that seeks to investigate a critical ontological site requires more than one genre of 'writing'. In other words, it uses more than one kind of 'text', calling upon reflexivity "enmeshed in power relations" (Ellingson, 2009, p. 10). We suggest the narratives created by Araki in this chapter provide such a text. As previously discussed, reflective journals or research logs can be written in a narrative form (such as the first narrative in this chapter). Alternatively, a new narrative piece can emerge from interpreting data based on raw data or combinations of the raw data (such as the second narrative in this chapter). 'Thus, a narrative analysis may both re-present the participant's narrative and also take interpretive authority for going beyond, in carefully documented ways, its literal and conscious meanings' (Josselson, 2011, p. 226). Following on from this assertion, Josselson (2011) provides useful suggestions for researchers constructing such an intricate space:

1. We do an overall reading of the interview to get a sense of how the narrative is structured and the general theme or themes. Then we return to each specific part to develop its meaning, and then consider the more global meanings in light of the deepened meaning of the parts.

2. We do multiple readings to identify different "voices" of the self and to create a view of how these selves are in dialogue with one another.

3. These iterative readings continue until we develop a "good Gestalt" that encompasses contradictions. The different themes make sensible patterns and enter into a coherent unity.

4. The work also enters into conversation with the larger theoretical literature so that the researcher can remain sensitive to nuances of meanings expressed and the different contexts into which the meanings may enter (p. 228).

The aim of working through the process is to gain 'an overall sense of meaning and then examining the parts in relation to it...[and to reach] a holistic understanding that best encompasses the meanings of the parts' (Josselson, 2011, p. 228). The holistic understanding cannot be achieved without discussing the reflexivity and the multi perspectives of self/selves in the narrative. The narrative piece introduced earlier in the chapter, which depicts Araki's first drama-based EFL class, clearly presents a multiplicity of self/selves. It included Araki as an empathetic researcher, an EFL teacher in Japan, a native to Japan who was once attended a primary school in Japan, an EFL teacher who taught in Australia, a bilingual person with intercultural understanding, a mother, and a member of the local community to name but a few. Narrative does not limit an individual as 'fixed in any representation of his or her words' (Josselson, 2011, p. 227). Analysing qualitative data with open forms like narrative can be a complex inquiry. O'Toole and Beckett (2010) stress the importance of recognising and accepting its complexity. In narratological terms this can be approached through a holistic or categorical form:

> 'In a holistic analysis, the life as represented in the narrative, is considered as a whole and sections of the text are interpreted with respect to the other parts. A categorical analysis abstracts sections or words belonging to a category, using coding strategies, and compares these to similar texts from other narratives. Maxwell (1996) refers to this distinction as one between contextualization and categorization. The dimension of *content versus form* refers to readings that concentrate on ether *what* is told or *how* it is told' (Josselson, 2011, p. 226).

Another approach suggested by O'Toole and Beckett (2010) is to look for connections—'something that makes the data coherent' (p. 170). Therefore, throughout the research inquiry the dialogic 'Wonderings' are in effect put to work in the anticipation to see, hear or understand something new.

Data Analysis as Representative Work

A Field Narrative from a Student's Perspective:

In the last drama-English class, we all became a hungry caterpillar and went shopping. I quite liked that activity. Araki sensei asked us to move like the caterpillar and think about how hungry the caterpillar was when shopping. Then, we decided how much food we bought. I crawled and wiggled my body to move forward on the floor until I got to the other side of the room where the shops were. It felt like it took ages to get there. We were all laughing because we all moved so differently. Being a customer at a caterpillar food shop was great as well. I couldn't remember how I should say some shopping words in English and I think I made some mistakes. I did remember 'apple please' and 'thank you'. I got what I wanted...I mean what the caterpillar wanted. I didn't worry about making mistakes so much and didn't feel embarrassed. We were too busy laughing and concentrating on being a caterpillar. Then, in today's class, Araki sensei asked us to draw food from a caterpillar's view. I remembered all the times in class when we became a caterpillar and her friends, family, and even the fruit and vegetables! It made drawing easy. Before we started drawing, we had a class discussion and talked about the size of the food if we were caterpillars. I decided to draw a grape. Just one grape. Because it must look so big in the caterpillar's eyes. I remembered the word 'through' from the caterpillar book, and we ate 'through' some fruit and vegetables in one of our mimes. You know to a tiny caterpillar, a grape must look huge 'cause it is much larger than the caterpillar's mouth or face.

I bought some grapes when I went shopping with my mum. I picked the best one and cut it into half. The inside looked so juicy and the colour was...light green, yellow, and green. Oh, I saw lots of lines. I held the half cut grape up to my eye—so this is what it is like to be a tiny caterpillar eating through it. I wouldn't have thought about looking at one tiny grape like this, inside and outside, unless I was asked to do such a drawing. (Araki 2005, translated field journal entry)

Incorporating the participants' voice in research brings more than students' prior-experience and understanding to the surface. The narrative above, like the others in this chapter, is constructed based on interview transcripts, research log written by teachers and the researcher, videotaped classes, students' written and oral feedback, and student drawings. The above foregrounds a story about the events that led to a student drawing a grape (see Image 1). Araki represents this particular student's responses to drama-based EFL classes by working and wondering *with/within* a range of data to paint and represent meaning in the research project. As Thomson (2008) explains, 'voice can mean not only having a say, but also refers to the language, emotional components and non-verbal means used to express opinions...[and]

the notion of voice suggests both a particular point of view, and also one which is not universal' (p. 4). Speaking *with* rather than speaking *for* the participants plays an important role in projects that seeks to address a radical collegiality (Fielding, 2004) in EFL research. As we have demonstrated, visual data and narratives can be most effective in the depiction of participants' learning. Eisner (1997) states that "…alternative forms of data representation can provide what might be called 'productive ambiguity'…that the material presented is more evocative than denotive, and in its evocation, it generates insight and invites attention to complexity" (p. 8). Of course these considerations must also be made while taking into account the intent, purpose and audiences of the research itself.

In education, narrative inquiry can draw out not only the complexities of participants' experiences, but it responds to the flexible nature of the inquiry by foregrounding the multiplicity of perception and interpretation of events or incidents. Therefore, "there is no single narrative inquiry method, but rather a number of methods… individual narrative inquiry approaches are typically combined with other methodological approaches and philosophies" (Webster and Mertova, 2007, p. 6). Because of its flexibility, there are cases where narrative inquiry is used as 'a reporting mechanism' (Webster and Mertova, 2007) within a case study, action research, auto-ethnography, and other qualitative research. In this chapter, we propose using narrative as both a form of analysis and representation. Like the narratives we have presented, they can be embedded in a project as both a process and a product of research (Araki, 2006) exemplifing analytical and dialogical work in EFL classrooms.

The following represents an example of how Araki turned a critical eye upon the experience of another Year 6 student to the caterpillar drawing task:

Drawing food from a caterpillar's view?! What does that mean? Araki sensei didn't show any examples of the kind of drawing she wanted. Tanaka sensei always gives us an example so that I know what he expects, but she just showed us white poster paper when she was explaining the activity. I wasn't even sure which way I should use…the white paper. I eventually went up to her and asked which way she wants us to use the paper, landscape or portrait. She said I could choose whichever I like… Whichever I like? Why can't she just tell me like Tanaka sen-

sei. He asked Araki sensei what she wanted us to to draw in our pictures and she said it is our choice. All she said was to choose food that a caterpillar could eat and we should draw from our caterpillar's perspective. Oh, and she wanted us to write the name of our food in English. Araki sensei gave us copies of a Japanese-English dictionary and said we can use them to look up words if we didn't know them. This is the very first time for me to learn English at school. Some of my classmates go to English conversation classes after school, but I only know the alphabet song. She also asked us to write what day of the week the caterpillar ate the food. I chose Monday because it looked easier to write and has less letters in it, if you compare it with other words like Wednesday! I think I copied it alright. What food should I draw? Araki sensei asked us to draw a background too. A tricky task, this one. I think she asks a lot. I wish she showed us some examples. My teacher later said we should all use crayons and water painting for the drawing. I decided to watch others draw for a while and then I will decide what I will draw. I am not good at this. What is the right choice? Am I doing it right? (Araki 2005, translated research journal entry)

Like the earlier student narrative, the above was pieced together from Araki's field notes, classroom discussions and conversations with the Year 6 teachers and students. Unexpected themes or new questions for future research may emerge when working *with/within* a range of data. For example, Araki's project suggested that further exploration about student autonomy and decision making with innovative classroom contexts may be needed in follow up projects on drama-based EFL in Japan (Araki, 2006).

Data Analysis as Responsive Work—Visual Data

Students' work samples including their visual work is valuable data although its significance is often supplanted in favour of the more traditional written or printed data. Stories reside just as evocatively in an image as they can within an interview transcript. The Drama-based EFL class provided an opportunity for Year 6 students to explore a fictional world of the caterpillar. Their drawings represented this experience and illustrated a conflation with their own everyday lives. Images 2, 3, 4 and 5 below reflect aspects of Japanese life that appeared in the caterpillar drawings. Based on Leitch's (2008) notion of a three-way dynamic engagement between researcher, participants and image in Araki's project exploration included not only language and language learning but also brought out critical cultural perceptions.

The original book of the very hungry caterpillar illustrates typical Western food, however, the students who drew Image 2, 3, and 4 chose to depict specifically typical and seasonal Japanese food. They did not simply replicate food from the original book. This was particularly significant as the hungry caterpillar is a very well known book and is available in Japanese (in fact some of the students were unaware that it was an American book). Their unfamiliar language, English, became much more familiar through participation in the drama based EFL class as it provided a unique opportunity for high level of engagement in language learning. Some students included regionally specific food—Image 2 is a famous local food in Fukuoka called *Mentaiko* (marinated fish egg with chili pepper). Their drawings demonstrated a sensibility towards seasonal food: each of Japan's four seasons has a culturally associated delicacy. The sweet dumplings in the cherry blossom season (Image 3) and chestnuts in Autumn (Image 4) are examples of such seasonal food. The final image 5, is a universal one but also a very commonplace food available in Japan. By participating in the drawing task, the students and teachers were drawn into discussions about what these foods meant to them and the role that these played in understanding themselves as Japanese and what 'Japanese' might mean in the broader globalized context. Ensuing decisions about why some foods had no English equivalent, why some foods were only had at particular times of the year, and why some foods were universal invited debate and questions about sustainability, nutrition and history into the class. The students' sense making and understanding of the world and their rich life experiences played an important part in the teaching and learning of this drama-based EFL class.

The drawing task itself and using the created images as a means of elaborating discussion in the research process disrupted typical EFL practice by "taking [teacher/researchers] into children's socio-emotional worlds outside the borders of normal classroom discourse and practice" (Leitch, 2008, p. 52). On one level Araki's disruption of expected roles and responsibilities by encouraging students to choose what and how to draw, led to the opportunity for some students to choose what and how to learn in this innovative ELF environment. Student experience is often neglected in typical

Monday

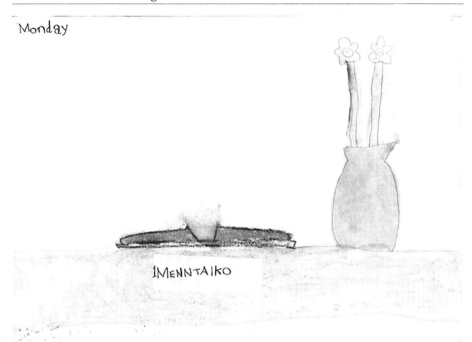

1MENNTAIKO

Tuesday.

cherrytree

One dumbling

EFL practice where teachers are often the acknowledged expert and the texts and language itself become the centre of attention. The affective, embodied and social life of the student are often secondary considerations. In such a research environment, valuing the visual image as data serves as a powerful voice to the hidden layers of the participants' understandings, experiences and life-worlds.

Concluding Remarks

月は満月よりも、幾分かけている方が風情がある。
(Tsukiha Mangetsu yori mo, ikubun kakete iru hoo ga fuzei ga aru—There is greater elegance in the partial moon than the full.) Sei Shoonagon, 2nd century female writer

We explored the generative nature of data and data analysis with several aims in mind in this chapter. A major concern was how we might engage with all research participants in such a way as to parallel the work of teaching and learning with the work of researching. It was also to consider how to focus on data and data analysis during the research process rather than an end product of a complete research project. Araki was able to work in a critically reflexive way attentive to emerging opportunities. In this chapter we have explored and discussed some of those issues raised by Araki's project. Our intent has been to make available to other EFL practitioner researchers the possibilities for investigating the nature of language learning and teaching within the everyday work of the classroom.

The nature of qualitative data is complex and responsive to the multiplicity of meanings in our social worlds and as Shoonagon points out, there is elegance to the imperfect or partial. With Kincheloe's encouragement in mind, we assert that there is much to be gained by engaging in a critical ontological practice during the 'doing' of research. In Araki's case, this lead to crystallisations of significant incidents with her co-participants as well as the forming and reforming of the relationships between all involved. In particular, one eloquent moment was when Araki stopped and paused over one of the students' drawings (Image 1). This fashioned and informed the life of the research and the pedagogy within the classroom. Students' work-samples and researchers' journals tend to be positioned as supportive data, not as generative data. This chapter may have provided an insight into what is possible and what might be useful for our colleagues eager to work beyond the usual and to make their work as teachers matter.

Dr. Naoko Araki
Faculty of Arts and Education
Deakin University

Dr. Kim Senior
Faculty of Arts and Education
Deakin University

References

Araki, N. (Araki-Metcalfe) (2006). The waterhole: Using educational drama as a pedagogical tool in a foreign language class at a public primary school in Japan, Ph.D. thesis, University of Melbourne, Australia.

Chase, S. (2011). Narrative inquiry: Still a field in the making. In Denzin, N., & Lincoln, Y. (eds.), *The SAGE Handbook of Qualitative Research*. London: SAGE.

Clandinin, J., & Connelly, M. (2000). *Narrative inquiry: experience and story in qualitative research*. San Francisco: Jossey-Bass.

Darder, A. (2002). *Reinventing Paulo Freire: A pedagogy of love*. Boulder: Westview Press.

Eisner, E. (1997). The promise and perils of alternative forms of data representation. *Educational Researcher 26*(6), 4-10.

Ellingson, L. (2009). *Engaging crystallization in qualitative research*. Thousand Oaks: Sage.

Fielding, M. (2004). Transformative approaches to student voice: Theoretical underpinnings. *Recalcitrant Realities' British Educational Research Journal 30*(2), 295-311.

Josselson. R. (2011). Narrative research: constructing, deconstructing and reconstructing story. In Werts, F. & Charmaz, K. et al. (eds.) *Five ways of doing qualitative analysis*. London: the Guilford Press.

Kincheloe. J. (2011). Critical ontology. In Hayes. K. et al. (eds.) *Key work in critical pedagogy: Joe L. Kincheloe* (pp. 201-217). Rotterdam: Sense Publishers.

Keegan, S. (2009). Improving interviewing (and other) skills. *Qualitative research: good decision making through understanding people, cultures, and market*. London: Kogan Page.

LeCompte, M. (2010). Analysing qualitative data. *Theory into Practice 39*(3), 146-154.

Leitch, R. (2008). Creatively researching children's narratives through images and drawings. In Thomson, P. (ed.) *Doing visual research with children and young people*. 4th ed. (pp. 37-58). Hoboken: Routledge.

O'Toole, J., & Beckett, D. (2009). *Educational research: creative thinking and doing*. South Melbourne: Oxford University Press.

Somekh, B. (1995). The contribution of action research to the development in social endeavours: a position paper on action research methodology. *British Educational Research Journal 21*(3), 339-355.

Thomson, P. (2008). Children and young people: Voices in visual research. In Thomson, P. (ed.) *Doing visual research with children and young people*. 4th ed. (pp. 1-19) Hoboken: Routledge.

Varga-Atkins, T., & O'Brien, M. (2009). From drawings to diagrams: maintaining researcher control during graphic elicitation in qualitative interviews. *International Journal of Research and Method in Education 32*(1), 53-67.

Webster, L., & Mertova, P. (2007). *Using narrative inquiry as a research method: an introduction to using critical event narrative analysis in research on learning and teaching*. London: Routledge

Chapter Eight

Positioning Oneself within EFL Research and Practice

A Cultural-Historical and Activity Theory View

ANNA POPOVA

This chapter will outline the position of a practitioner/researcher within the context of EFL teaching and learning from a cultural-historical and activity theory (CHAT) perspective. The selection of this theoretical perspective is based on the growing importance of CHAT in the field of education in general and EFL in particular. CHAT articulates an ethical and modern position of a practitioner who is not reflective as an individual only, but who is part of the collective and cultural praxis of where EFL teaching and learning occur. The Praxis of English Language Learning and Teaching (PELT) is part of the cultural, historical and social reality in which the practitioner operates, and therefore the very nature of the learning and teaching processes yields itself to the adoption of a CHAT approach. Another reason for selecting these theoretical lenses is my own cultural and professional trajectory. I was trained as a teacher of the EFL in Russia, where CHAT concepts, being primarily based on Vygotsky's ideas (1978, 1986), are represented in the educational practices and methods. I will use examples of learning and teaching EFL in the context of post-soviet Russia. In addition, I have used CHAT in a number of research projects and I will draw on this experience, too.

M. Vicars et al. (eds.), *The Praxis of English Language Teaching and Learning (PELT)*, 141–157.

The chapter will provide the reader with a CHAT conceptual apparatus, which will allow them to use these concepts in everyday research practice. This will allow the reader to be able to analyse the context in which they are conducting their practice. The chapter will provide an argument that it is through the analysis of systemic contradictions and careful analysis of existing power structures, that the practitioner/researcher can conduct critical research respectfully. Finally, I will then argue for EFL research being a relational matter by explaining how a practitioner/researcher can reformulate their positioning and develop relational agency.

It is important to notice that the CHAT tradition is long and complex. The aim of the chapter is to use CHAT concepts to help an EFL practitioner/researcher, and not to provide a comprehensive account of CHAT complexity. As this whole volume aims at exploring liberating forms of researching in PELT, the CHAT framework is discussed here as a way of thinking and acting in the name of social justice. As Stetsenko (2012, p. 147) eloquently puts it:

> Explicitly grounded in Marxist philosophy and profoundly saturated with goals of a radical social transformation, Vygotsky's theory stands out even today in its philosophical depth, conceptual breadth, and clear ideological commitment to social justice.

Situating the Researcher as a Practitioner

Situating oneself both as a researcher and practitioner is an old notion. It has been explored in the writing associated with approaches such as action research (Stringer, 2007), reflective practice (Ghaye, 2010), praxis inquiry (Burridge et al., 2010) and work based research (Costley, Elliot & Gibbs, 2011), to mention just a few. Yet, the issue which is often discussed vaguely is about the definition of practice, praxis or work. For example, Costley, Elliot and Gibbs (2011) use the terms work based environment, work based context and practice almost interchangeably. They discuss the benefits and methods of researching one's own practice at one's own place of work, yet the definition of what it is that researchers are engaged in, and what is understood by the notions of environment or practice is not clear. Some recommendations within action research tradition ask to locate a problem that needs to be solved within the practice that requires an action. But the question that remains unanswered is about the boundaries of this practice and criteria used for locating ourselves within our own practice. For EFL practitioners/researchers it may be interesting to reflect whether their practice is located within the classroom and institution boundaries, or whether it stretches to cultural, national and temporal demarcations. It is important to question whether their critical pedagogy tackles immediate issues created by people they interact with or it deals with deep systemic contradictions that have emerged over the course of history. In this section, I will explore some fundamental CHAT concepts that can help demarcate how far or deep we can go when positioning ourselves as a researcher/practitioner.

What am I Working On?

One of the major challenges a practitioner/researcher may experience is to locate the actual focus of the practice they have joined. It is especially pertinent if they teach EFL in a country where English is not the first language, and if they themselves come from somewhere else. Traditionally, it is suggested that teachers of EFL adapt to the new situation and listen to their students, as well as respond to their individual needs (Erlam & Gray, 2012). These recommendations are valid and maybe helpful, and yet, they do not help practitioners analyse the nature of the practice they have joined.

In the CHAT tradition, it is argued that everything that humans do, they do within a culturally mediated activity. Vygotsky (1978) proposed that we do not automatically and directly respond to any stimulus from the environment, but act on whatever the reality presents through the prism of previously acquired cultural artefacts which include culturally specific concept-formations and values (see figure 8.1).

These ideas have been extensively discussed by the two prominent scholars in EFL research, for example Lantolf (2006) and Thorne (2009). They have explored processes of cultural mediation in the second language (L2) teaching and learning context. For example, Lantolf (2006) discussed whether L2 can become a cultural artefact that could mediate the learners' thinking. Yet, in this chapter, I would like to focus more on the practitioner's awareness and skills of analysing, exploring and researching the practice in

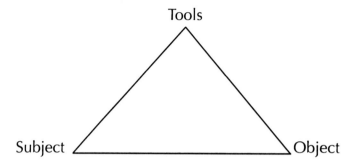

Fig. 8.1 Model of cultural mediation adapted from Daniels et al. (2005, p. 84)

which they are involved, without necessarily looking closely at particular artefacts or teaching processes. In other words, the argument in this chapter encourages practitioners to analyse their practice from, what I call, a 'helicopter view', and explore their social, cultural and relational positions within the PELT context.

Thus, the main concern of the practitioner/researcher in PELT is to understand what it is that the community they have joined are working on. If it is not in the country of their own, the process is extremely complex. A.N. Leontiev, the creator of activity theory argued that when humans act, they act within culturally and historically established systems, which has got its own rules and traditions.

> Activity [in its generic sense] is the nonadditive, molar unit of life for the material, corporeal subject. In a narrower sense (i.e., on the psychological level) it is the unit of life that is mediated by mental reflection. The real function of this unit is to orient the subject in the world of objects. In other words, activity is not a reaction or aggregate of reactions, but a system with its own structure, its own internal transformations, and its own development (Leontiev, 1979, p. 46).

Stetsenko (2012, p.148) elaborates on the original definition of an activity, by emphasising the ongoing nature of an individual's embeddedness in it.

This new relation to the world, precisely as a new form of life (Lebensweise)—
the sociocultural collaborative transformative practice that unfolds and gradually
expands in time—in essence brings about the emergence of human beings and
constitutes the foundation for their development in all its expressions and facets.

Leontiev, further argues that an activity is defined by an object-motive—
something that the participants of the activity are working on, shaping,
modifying and transforming. Daniels et al. (2007, p. 523) state that "The
object is the constantly reproduced purpose of a collective activity system
that motivates and defines the horizon of possible goals and actions". Object-
motives are quite stable and difficult to transform because they are linked
to the development of individuals' consciousness. Leontiev (1978) argues
that individuals operate with a hierarchy of object-motives, which means
sometimes object-motives come into conflict with each other. This may explain why when we try to teach our students to use English to converse or
interpret information (which has been the object of Western education for
a while now), the students maybe focusing on something else, for example,
trying to acquire knowledge of grammar from your lesson. So, you might
be working on their skills of using language for communication, and they
may be working on decoding the structure of the language. In the context of
teaching English in Russia, this might be precisely the case. Traditionally, the
teaching of Russian, the native language, focuses on the structural, as well
as stylistic aspects of the language. This has been translated into the methodologies of teaching EFL. In my experience, attempts to change the focus
and methods of teaching for students who have been educated in the Soviet
Union are not very successful. I remember trying to teach a group of mature
students by using a Cambridge framework of teaching and Cambridge EFL
resources. I struggled to involve students in dialogues. My students, as it
happened, wanted to know how the language worked overall, rather than
use limited vocabulary and sentence structure to converse.

Thus, the partitioner/researcher in PELT might experience what Leontiev called a conflict of objects. Leontiev emphasizes that an individual alone
might not be able to resolve this conflict because the ordering of which
object-motive is more important is based on how we make sense of the
cultural meanings generated within a particular activity; and the activity as

self-directed system may exert power over individuals. This happens because individuals themselves are more drawn to work on the culturally-historically established object-motives. In the example, above, I tried to involve students into an activity that did not really exist in their reality, at least not with the object-motive they were working on. It is important to note that once I reverted back to the focus on the structure of the language and analytical tasks that helped unpack grammar structures, I could see that my students were progressing much faster in acquiring vocabulary and being able to use English in communication.

In order to grasp what the object-motive of the activity you have joined is, you need to learn about the culture of the country in which you teach, and also any available information about EFL teaching and learning in that country, as well as an overall focus of education. This is a very difficult process because the information that you need is usually published in the language of that country in practice-oriented journals or practitioner manuals. One way of overcoming this is to find out whether there are locally published manuals and learning materials that you can get hold of. Analysing those may help you in understanding what the overall object-motive of the EFL cultural-historical activity has been. It is also good to talk to the local EFL practitioners and explore their views about the priorities they see in teaching EFL, and also the ways in which they see their learners.

Systemic View of a Cultural-Historical Activity

Although the CHAT tradition dictates clearly that it in order to participate in an activity that you are not familiar with, you need to identify its object, it also implies that an activity is some kind of system. Only at the end of the twentieth century, a Finnish Professor Y. Engeström (1987, 1990, and 1999) articulated that idea both theoretically and methodologically. He expanded the original triangular model of cultural mediation (figure 8.1) by indicating the ways in which mediation is linked to a number of other factors (figure 8.2). He explained that in the modern world we need to take into account that an activity will have an impact outside its boundaries, and therefore a wider community with which a subject is working needs to be identified; systemic contradictions (rules) are described in this model as linked to other

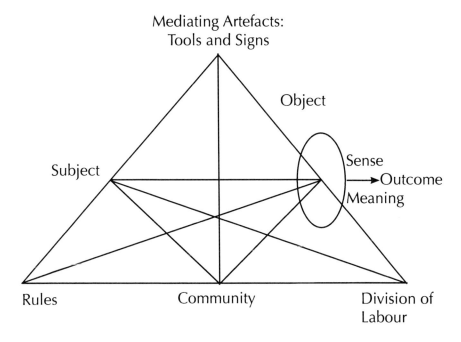

The structure of a human activity system
Engeström 1987 p.78

*Fig. 8.2 Expanded model of an activity, adapted from Daniels et al.
(2005, p. 85).*

components of the system in a dynamic way; and finally, he proposed the idea of 'division of labour' which defines the ways in which power is distributed within the system. An activity system, therefore, emerged as a unit of analysis within cultural-historical research by providing clear boundaries and categories of analysis.

For a PELT researcher this model can be a useful tool for defining what kind of practice they are entering and identifying some ways of locating their position within this system. From a structural point of view a PELT researcher can ask questions with regard to each element of the system:

- **Subject:** Who is doing the work? Is it I, the practitioner, or is it my students?

- **Object:** Are we working on the same thing?

- **Tools:** What ideas of education/languages learning guide my students' learning? What educational/pedagogical ideas guide my way of teaching? Is there a clash?

- **Rules:** How does PELT fit into an organisational structure of the institution where I teach? For example, is the teaching of English perceived to be a post-colonial endeavour, and therefore, may clash with the overall object of education (liberation from colonialism)?

- **Community:** Who else, apart from the obvious players (students and teachers) have a say in the teaching and learning process? Who funds the course? Who are you accountable to?

- **Division of Labour:** Who holds the power in the teaching and learning process? Do you make decisions about what is best for the students? Or are the students in the driving seat of the learning process? Perhaps, it is neither you nor the students, but the managerial staff of the organisation where you work who dictate what should happen within an education process.

So, as a result of the analysis of the activity system within which you work, you might realise that you are just one of the tools of the learning and teaching process, i.e. that you deliver the teaching through the methods and ideas that do not come from your own view of PELT; or you might realise that you hold all the power which is due to the need of your students to acquire a high proficiency in English. When I look back at my own EFL training which took place at the end of the 1990s in Russia, I can clearly see that the activity system within which I was learning English was not limited by the boundaries of PELT. The teacher training University where I was studying incorporated deep seated rules of Soviet education into the very core of its functioning. Thus, the division of labour was extremely clearly demarcated; the teaching staff held very firmly formulated ideas of how to teach EFL as a degree, and the students had to follow that model, or leave the system. In the competitive labour market of post-Soviet Russia, students did not see a way of making their voice heard, despite the fact that they could see that some of the ideas and teaching methods were politically and socially out-dated.

Creating Transformations through Research

Challenges Emerging After the Analysis of an Activity System

Whatever is the result of your activity system analysis, you might end up facing a number of practice related challenges. You might realise that the challenge is related to the nature or the ways in which 'tools' are used within an activity system. Perhaps, it is a matter of you bringing in your pedagogical tool-box to a classroom in a culture you are unfamiliar with. This may be revealed in your students not being able to understand the relevance of the task you give them, or in fact, the task itself. You can also face the challenge of realising that you seem to be persuading your students to 'buy into' your ways of doing things, and that they seem to be 'silently resisting'. You might also face a challenge of not sharing the object of the activity. I remember that during my training, a British lecturer joined the staff of our English faculty. This was the first 'native' speaking person that my peer-students and I saw in our life and we were excited to learn from her. We were greatly surprised, though, that during the first session with us, she asked us to read a short text and discuss it in small groups. She then left the room, and came back when she thought we must have finished the task. At it happened we had not started reading or discussing the text. The whole idea of reading something in class (as different from reading a text as home-work) and then discussing it only with other two or three people (as different from the whole class discussion) was so unfamiliar to us that we honestly did not know what to do. From an activity theory perspective, the British lecturer was focussing on our interpretive skills in using English, whereas we were focusing on 'training' ourselves in using English. She wanted us to 'pick up' ideas from the text and then add what we have gained from the text to our already evolving language structure; whereas we had always worked in the system where our lectures made very clear where to position the new information or new vocabulary in the overall structure of the English language.

Expansive Learning in PELT

So, when such challenges have been identified, it is difficult to find the right solution. Thus, for example, in the example above, the British lecturer in the Russian higher education context might have considered a number of solutions. One of those might have been a decision to adapt to the existing system and adopt the teaching methods used by the Russian lecturers. Another solution could have been to try and integrate British concepts of teaching EFL into the activity system. Both solutions would have been challenging. The former solution would have required her to change her whole view of teaching and learning teaching skills which she had been acquiring for a while. The second solution would have required all the staff to make changes in their practice, and change the curriculum, without really seeing the reason to do so.

Engeström (2005) proposed a methodological approach that was designed to resolve such challenges. His argument was predicated on Vygotsky's original method of inquiry called 'double stimulation'. This means that instead of expecting participants of the research to react to a stimulus, it is necessary to present them with a secondary stimulus that would mediate their thinking and action. In terms of modern research scenarios, this meant that the participants had to have a tool for analysing their own practice and realising what deep-seated contradictions might have prevented them from being more successful or effective. Engeström proposed the idea of a change laboratory, a series of workshops, where participants of the same activity or several related activities had an opportunity to analyse their practice through the lenses of the activity theory model. The triangular model itself became the second stimulus necessary for the participants to make changes they deemed necessary. Although, this methodological approach grew in popularity as an intervention methodology, and has been applied to a variety of social contexts, it has proved to be an expensive and time consuming process. It required a researcher from an outside of an organisation to work with a group of people over a long period of time; the result could only be achieved of the participants were committed to the research programme. This can be challenging for a practitioner/researcher whose immediate priority is to teach a group of students.

Yet, the underlying principles of this methodological approach can be extremely useful for PELT researchers. Engeström argued that the purpose of the intervention methodology was expansive learning', i.e. "the capacity of participants in an activity to interpret and expand the definition of the object of activity and respond to it in increasingly enriched ways" (Daniels et al. 2007, p. 523). In PELT contexts, practitioners might need to take a decision of who will be involved in this transformative work, students or other practitioners. Due to the nature of the PELT (that may occur far from the practitioner's own organisation or can take a short period of time, as in a case of a short intensive EFL course), it might not be possible to involve other practitioners into expansive learning. However, I suggest that it is realistic to use the idea of expansive learning and the double stimulation method as a way of both continuing to participate in practice and transforming this practice at the same time. Expansive learning can become both a teaching tool and a research method. I suggest that in PELT students might be encouraged to think about the reasons behind some of the teaching methods used in the classroom, to be asked to think of how a particular task might help them reach their own goals in learning English. Contradictions within the system that are usually not talked about need to be laid bare and discussed openly. Going back to the example which involved a British tutor in a Russian University, it can be argued that a discussion with the students about a different approach in learning and teaching, might have given the students a different challenge, and we might have been more conscious of the reasons why were asked to carry out that particular task.

Co-configuration and 'Knot-working' as Possible Research Aims

If other practitioners are in an organisation are to be involved into the process of the transformation of the activity, then the aims of the transformation have to be clear. It is traditional to consider organisational transformations as processes that involve organisation restructuring or changes in management systems. Often, changes are made when a new policy or curriculum are introduced. However, here I focus on the changes that can happen in the practice of practitioners/researchers who teach EFL either in their home organisation with a group of students who come from different language backgrounds, or in an organisation away from their home country, where students will come from the same language background. Yet, the changes that can be made will affect more than just the classroom practice of the researcher/practitioner; there will be shifts in the activity system overall.

The activity system will not change if it still operates with olds ways of thinking and acting. What needs to happen is for new ideas to be gradually introduced into the system through carefully managed collaboration with the others. In the CHAT based research I was involved before (Daniels et. al. 2007; e.g. Broughton, 2005), apart from the idea of expansive learning, the interventions we carried out were guided by two other concepts, namely co-configuration and 'knot-working'. Below, I will expand on both of these ideas and explain how these can be applied to PELT research.

The idea of co-configuration comes from the work of Victor and Boynton (1998). They reflected upon historical forms of work, and argued that historically, creation of a product or service began with craft work; it went through the process of mass production and then towards mass customisation. At the level of craft, work is intuitive and knowledge is tacit. In EFL classes this can still be evident when practitioners use their unique 'toolbox' of methods, and they cannot explain why these methods are effective. During the process of mass customisation, on the other hand, methods that were developed through craft work, were then mass produced are then packaged into a product that is suitable for everybody. This way, for example, a Cambridge English course is delivered in similar ways, irrespective of whether it is in Holland, Mauritius or Russia.

Victor and Boynton (1998) argue that it is no longer effective to offer customers the same product and that the product needs to be co-configured. This process involves "an attempt to adapt practices in order to respond to the changing needs of clients and to involve clients in co-designing the services they receive" (Daniels et al. 2007, p. 525). Co-configuration process does not have an end; it is continuous and is always evolving. This means that in EFL contexts it is impossible to conceive of a course, unit or module that can be delivered in the same form to different audiences. In activity theory terms, in each cultural context, we need to identify the object that the participants think they are working on and adapt the 'tools' with which we think we will be working on the object. This is where it is important to think of an activity system as an open system, which can be slightly re-shaped. In PELT, 'units' or courses of teaching and learning have to be open enough, so that they can be co-configured in the context after the activity system has been analysed, and participants of the activity system have had a chance to analyse the system and together with the practitioner find ways of shaping the teaching and learning process in the ways most suitable to the cultural context and local expectations. In a way, co-configuring means co-creating together, on the basis of open negotiation of what needs to be done, acquired, learnt, produced, etc.

Of course, it is difficult to co-configure the teaching and learning pro-cess when practitioners work in the environment where there are no stable teams. The colleagues they work with might be employed at that institution on a temporary basis, or the practitioners themselves come to teach only one course (for example, teaching an EFL unit as part of a University's overseas programme). In situations like this, it is not possible to rely on collective memory and established ways of net-working, which occurs within tradi-tional teams. Thus, Engeström (2005, p. 98) suggested an idea of 'knot-working', defined as follows:

> We have encountered numerous examples of work organisations in which collabo-ration between the partners is of vital importance, yet takes shape without strong pre-determined rules or central authority. I call such forms of collaborative work 'knotworking'. The notion of knot refers to rapidly pulsating, distributed and par-tially improvised orchestration of collaborative performance between otherwise loosely connected actors and organisational units. Knotworking is characterized by a movement of tying, untying and retying together seemingly separate threads of activity.

The most important aspect of knotworking is that it is not necessarily linked to large organisational changes. Knotworking is a way of creating temporary teams that can work on a particular aspect of an activity. It is a form of work-ing where the participants involved are aware of the deep contradictions in the activity system, and consciously try to work on expansive learning. Inside and EFL classroom, knotworking implies bringing in the students' strengths and particular expertise, as well as certain cultural expectations to co-configure what needs to be learnt. This may involve making some aspects of learning explicit, and often let the students direct the way the learning goes. In order to achieve this, practitioners need to acquire a different view of relational research/practice, which is discussed below.

Research as Relational Matter

One the of major issues with conducting research in education practice is using concepts of the 'self', individual development or identity that do not really reflect other aspects of the research. Using incompatible concepts for the analysis of practice and the self lies may bring inconsistency in understanding what is going on in the classroom or the whole institution. So, if in CHAT terms, we see practice as dynamic process which is deeply rooted in the ways people have been constructing it over a long period of time, then we need a concept of the self and relationship with others that reflects that idea. The CHAT researchers have been working on a relational notion of an individual, which is rooted in the socio-cultural activity in which individuals are involved. Some refer to this as personhood (from Russian 'lichnost'). As an EFL practitioner/researcher you need to think about how you see your students, yourself, other practitioners and the relationship among all the actors. It is habitual to think of students in the classroom as unique individuals who have brought with them the richness of their previous experience. We talk about meeting individual needs and following individual interests. Stetsenko (2012, p.145) criticises some of these approaches:

> What is common to these views is that they celebrate a certain sort of person who, firstly, is at the whim of powerful forces outside of one's control and even awareness, and thus can hardly expect or be expected to act purposefully and responsibly. Secondly, this is a solitary, autonomous individual not only unrelated and unattached to others but in constant antagonism with them, impelled to avoid and resist social forces that are intrinsically alien to human "primordial nature".

CHAT does not deny the idea of an individual's uniqueness but it emphasises that this uniqueness comes from the fact that individuals are constructing themselves and others through participating in an activity. Russian psychologist Dodonov (1985, also cited in Popova 2009) proposed that studies of practices and individuals ought to complement each other. He stressed that the concept of personhood should find a balanced position between them. Dodonov suggested considering the relationship between the social and individual as a function of personhood. Each function should be viewed as part of society. According to Dodonov, personhood and society belong to the same class of self-organising systems. Personhood is defined as a "self-organising, purpose-oriented 'part of society'; its general function lies in re-alising an individual way of social being" (Dodonov, 1985, p. 37). Stetsenko (2012, p. 151) takes it even further:

> The core difference is that positing transformative collaborative practice at the core of human development suggests that this development is an active and even activist project of a historical Becoming aimed at contributing to common human history. In relational ontology, a person is embedded in the social world and is a special kind of agent for whom things have characteristically human significance—for whom things matter (cf. Sugarman, 2005). From the activist transformative stance outlined herein, however, persons are agents not only for whom "things matter" but who themselves matter in history, culture, and society and, moreover, who come into Being as unique individuals through and to the extent that they matter in these processes and make a contribution to them.

This implies that upon or during the analysis of an activity system, practitioners/ researchers will encounter relational paths and trajectories, which do not only affect both parties but the activity which is being analysed. When we explore PELT with an aim to create a context where a language is learnt in a way that best suits to the individual path of development, we also co-configure the activity in which this learning is being acquired. The co-configured activity gives opportunities for exploring how personhood's functioning can be transformed, for the practitioner is not located within oneself, and the student is not located within themselves either; it is through participation, join-analysis and co-configuration of the teaching/learning activity that both parties explore their own uniqueness. Therefore, the questions within the framework proposed in this chapter cannot be aimed at improving the delivery of a course or strengthening teaching and learning aims. Instead, the focus is on how best to activate the personhood of those involved in what Stetsenko (2012) calls an activist project of historical becoming.

Conclusion

In this chapter I proposed a framework for conducting research in PELT. Rooted in the cultural-historical activity theory, this framework is argued to assist practitioners/researchers in a conscious act of analysing deep-seated contradictions of the activity within which they find themselves working. Research and practice are interconnected processes but not inseparable. It is extremely important while adopting a CHAT approach to have time to collect necessary information about the activity system in which practitioners work, and have some reflection time for the analysis. Yet, due the fact that relational aspects of this kind of research practice are predicated upon an idea that participants actively change themselves while they are changing the activity itself, it is important to ensure that participants are aware of the practitioner's endeavour to understand practice and negotiate innovative learning paths. The aims of this kind of research is not to find solutions that can be used as ready-made products delivered world-wide. Instead, CHAT research within PELT can serve to re-structure and re-configure existing teaching and learning pathways. Thus, whether it is the power imbalance, or the use of incompatible tools in teaching, or the different perspective of the same activity that the partitioner has found through the CHAT analysis, actions on the basis of such research will lead to a more liberating practice—the practice that has potential for continuous development.

Dr Anna Popova
Faculty of Education and Arts
Australian Catholic University

References

Broughton, K. (2005). Research into practice: The national evaluation of The Children's Fund. practice. *Social Work in Action 17*(2), 135-139.

Burridge, P., Carpenter, C., Cherednichenko, B. & Kruger, T. (2010). Investigating praxis inquiry within teacher education using Giddens' structuration theory. *Journal of Experimental Education 33*(1), 19-37.

Costley, C., Elliott, G. & Gibbs, P. (2010). *Doing work-based research: approaches to enquiry for insider-researchers.* London: SAGE.

Daniels. H. (2001). *Vygotsky and pedagogy.* London: Routledge.

Daniels, H., Brown, S., Edwards, A., Leadbetter, J., Middleton, D., Parsons, S., Popova, A. & Warmington, P. (2005). Studying professional learning for inclusion. In K. Yamazumi, Y. Engestrom & H. Daniels (Eds.), *New learning challenges: going beyond the industrial age system of school and work* (pp. 79-103). Osaka: Kansai University Press.

Daniels, H., Leadbetter, J., Warmington, P., Edwards, A., Martin, D., popova, A., Apostolov, A., Middleton, D. & Brown, S. (2007). Learning in and for Multi-agency Working. *Oxford Review of Education 33*(4), 521-538.

Dodonov, B.I. (1985). O sisteme 'lichnost'. [About the system of personhood]. *Voprosi Psihologii, 5,* 36-45.

Engeström, Y. (1987). *Learning by expanding: an activity theory—theoretical approach to developmental research.* Helsinki: Orienta–Konsultit.

Engeström, Y. (1990). *Learning, working and imagining: Twelve studies in activity theory.* Helsinki: Orienta: Konsultit.

Engeström, Y. (1999). Activity theory and individual and social formation. In Y. Engeström, R. Miettinen, R. Punamäki (Eds.). *Perspectives on activity theory* (pp. 19-39). Cambridge: Cambridge University Press.

Engeström, Y. (2001). Expansive learning at work: towards an activity theoretical reconceptualisation. *Journal of Education and Work 14*(1), 133-156.

Engeström, Y. (2005). *Developmental work research: Expanding activity theory in practice.* Vol. 12. Berlin: Docupoint Madgeburg.

Erlam, R. & Gray, S. (2012). 'Reconseptualizing' self as a teacher in a Malaysian context. In T. Muller, S. Herder, J. Adamson & P.S. Brown (eds.) *Innovating EFL teaching in Asia*, (pp. 110-123). London: Palgrave Macmillan.

Ghaye, T. (2010). *Teaching and learning through reflective practice: A practical guide for positive action.* London & New York: Routledge.

Lantolf, J.P. (2006). Sociocultural Theory and L2. State of the Art. *SSLA*, Viol. 28, 67-109.

Leontiev, A.N. (1978). *Activity, consciousness and personality.* (M.J. Hall, Trans.). Englewood Cliffs, NJ.: Prentice-Hall. (Original work published 1975)

Leontiev, A.N. (1979). The problem of activity in psychology. In J.V. Wertch (Ed. and Trans.), *The concept of activity in Soviet psychology* (pp. 37-71). Armonk, NY: Sharpe.

Popova, A. (2009). *Socio-cultural and activity theory analysis of preparation for work in Russian schools.* A thesis submitted for the degree of Doctor of Philosophy, University of Bath, Department of Education.

Stetsenko, A. (2012). Personhood: An activist project of historical becoming through collaborative pursuits of social transformation. *New Ideas in Psychology 30*,144-153.

Stringer, E.T. (2007). *Action Research.* Los Angeles: SAGE.

Thorne, S.L. (2009). 'Community', semiotic flows, and mediated contribution to activity. *Language Teaching 42*(1), 81-94.

Victor, B. & Boynton, A. (1998). Invented here: maximazing your organization's internal growth and profitability. Boston: Harvard Business School Press.

Vygotsky, L. S. (1986). *Thought and language.* (A. Kozulin, ed. and trans.). Massachusetts: The M.I.T. Press. (original work published in 1934)

Vygotsky, L. S. (1978). *Mind in society.* (M. Cole, John-Steiner, V., Scribner, S. & Souberman, E., Eds.). Cambridge: Harvard University Press.

About the Contributors

Naoko Araki was a Senior Lecturer in LOTE/TESOL at Deakin University, Australia. She has taught at a tertiary level both in Australia and Japan. She studied at The University of Melbourne in the 90s as an international student and later taught Japanese at schools in Australia and English in Japan. Her research interests are pedagogical relationships and theorising integrated curriculum with applied theatre in additional language education.

Marcelle Cacciattolo is a sociologist and an Associate Professor in the College of Education at Victoria University, Melbourne Australia. She received her PhD from Monash University in 2002. Over the last decade her research has been cross-disciplinary involving health sciences and education-based research. Other research projects that Marcelle has been involved in include young people and their wellbeing, refugee relocation, social justice and authentic teaching and learning pedagogies within tertiary settings. Marcelle is a senior researcher in the Standpoint project and works closely with schools in the Western Region to examine how inclusive pedagogies can support children and families who are the least advantaged. Marcelle teaches in both undergraduate and postgraduate units in the College of Education.

Domenica Maviglia is Doctor of Philosophy in intercultural pedagogy at the Department of Cognitive Science, Education, and Cultural Studies of the University of Messina. Her work focuses mainly on critical pedagogy and the theoretical and historical research in the field of pedagogy, with a particular emphasis on the philosophy of education, the history of pedagogy, and the history of education. In her career, she has worked with different educational and training institutions, taking part to educational research projects carried out in several schools. Among her publications are *Joe Lyons Kincheloe's Critical Pedagogy.* In Porfilio, B. J., Ford, D. R. (2014) *Leaders in Critical Pedagogy.* Boston: Sense; *Educare alla criticità. Fondamenti storici e linee di sviluppo della Critical Pedagogy di Joe Lyons Kincheloe.* (Educate to criticise: historical foundations and development possibilities of Joe Lyons Kincheloe's Critical Pedagogy) Messina: Bertone, 2011; *L'azione critica della parola nell'esperienza pedagogica di don Milani.* (The critical power of the word in the pedagogical experience of Don Milani). Quaderni di Intercultura, DOI 10.3271/A19, pp. 31-36; *The Historical Origins of Critical Pedagogy in the Theory of Joe Lyons Kincheloe.* In Brock, R., Villaverde, L., Mallot, C. (Eds) (2011). *Teaching Kincheloe.* New York: Peter Lang; *Una nuova frontiera del bullismo: il Cyberbullismo.* (The new frontier of bullying: cyber-bullying). In Sirna, C., Michelin Salomon, A. (2009) *Bullismo protagonismo anomalo.* (Bullying; strange protagonist). Lecce: Pensa Multimedia; *La legislazione per gli stranieri in Italia dall'Unità ad Oggi.* (Law for foreigners in Italy, from the Unification of Italy to the Present Day). In Hamburger, F., Sirna, C. (edited by) (2008), *Interculturalità come progetto politico e come pratica pedagogica.* (Interculturalism as political project and pedagogical practice). Lecce: Pensa Multimedia.

Tarquam McKenna is a Professor at Victoria University, Melbourne, Australia. Dr McKenna has been active as a Teacher Educator and an Arts Psychotherapist for thirty years. He is immediate past president of The Association for Qualitative Research (AQR) and an honorary life member of the Australian and New Zealand Art Therapy Association. He is keenly interested in educational research methods, social justice and especially research approaches using artful practices. His work especially focuses on the use of praxis inquiry approaches to redress the lifeworld challenges of the least advantaged communities.

Anna Popova is currently working at Australian Catholic University in Melbourne as Senior Lecturer in Early Childhood Education. Her career in education has spanned over 20 years, which includes teaching in primary schools, conducting research in educational contexts and lecturing in early childhood. Her interest and expertise in socio-cultural and activity theory take roots in her education in Russia. Applying the theory in her PhD research in the UK has deepened the interest in it and she has been using its concepts in a variety of research contexts since. English is the second language for Anna. She is intrigued by the complexities of the teaching and learning of foreign languages.

Kim Senior is Senior Lecturer in Pedagogy and Curriculum at Deakin University, Melbourne, Australia. She has over two decades experience as an educator in Australia, Vietnam and Japan. She lived in Japan in the early 1980's as an exchange student in Kyushu and later studied at Okayam University. She has taught Japanese in Australia at both secondary and tertiary level. Her research interests focus upon pedagogical relationships, literacies and visual methodology/methods in research.

Shirley R. Steinberg is Research Professor of Youth Studies, formerly the Werklund Foundation Chair and the Director of the Werklund Foundation Centre for Youth Leadership Studies at the University of Calgary. She is the co-founder and director of The Paulo and Nita Freire International Project for Critical Pedagogy. She is the author and editor of many books in critical literacies, critical pedagogy, urban and youth culture, and cultural studies. Her most recent books include: *Critical Youth Studies* (2014) and *The Critical Qualitative Research Reader* (2012). She is currently finishing two books: *Writing and Publishing* (Fall 2015) and *The Bricolage and Qualitative Research* (Fall 2015). A regular contributor to CBC Radio One, CTV, *The Toronto Globe and Mail*, *The Montreal Gazette*, and *Canadian Press*, she is also a weekly columnist for CTVNEWS Channel on Culture Shock. The organizer of The International Institute for Critical Pedagogy and Transformative Leadership, she is committed to a global community of transformative educators and community workers engaged in radical love, social justice, and the situating of power within social and cultural contexts.

Mark Vicars is Senior Lecturer in Literacy in the College of Education at Victoria University, Melbourne, Australia. Mark has worked as a literacy educator in Japan, Korea, Thailand, Vietnam, Cambodia, England, and Australia. An overarching concern of his work is the connectivities between literacy and identity practices in everyday life.

Anthony Watt is Senior Lecturer in the College of Education at Victoria University. His research work is in the areas of the design and development of assessment instruments in sport psychology, student engagement in physical education, and childhood physical activity. His teaching focuses on the key practices associated with the teaching of physical education at the primary and secondary school levels. He has supervised nine doctoral theses to completion and has published two books, three book chapters and 30 journal articles in the area of physical education, motor control, physical activity, and sport psychology.

CPSIA information can be obtained at www.ICGtesting.com
Printed in the USA
LVOW10s0819010615

440675LV00003B/6/P

9 789463 001106